THE AUTHENTIC LEADER AS SERVANT (ALS)

ALS I COURSE 2
DISCIPLESHIP LEADERSHIP
Attributes, Principles, and Practices

SYLVANUS N. WOSU, Ph.D

THE AUTHENTIC LEADER AS SERVANT
ALS I COURSE 2
Discipleship Leadership Attributes, Principles, and Practices

© Copyright 2024 by Sylvanus N. Wosu Ph.D.

Printed in the United States of America
ISBN: 978-8-9863274-4-0

All rights reserved. No part of this book may be reproduced or transmitted in any form or by any means, electronic or mechanical, including photocopying, recording, or by any information storage and retrieval system, without permission in writing from the copyright owner.

Bible quotations are from the New King James (NKJV) version of the Bible unless otherwise indicated.

Other versions used in this book are the New International Version (NIV), New Living Translation (NLT), King James Version (KJV), English Standard Version (ESV), and Good News Translation (GNT). Unless otherwise specified, NKJV should be assumed.

The views expressed in this work are solely those of the author and do not necessarily reflect the views of the publisher, and the publisher disclaims any responsibility for them.

To order additional copies of this book, contact:
Proisle Publishing Services LLC
39-67 58th Street, 1st floor
Woodside, NY 11377, USA
Phone: (+1 646-480-0129)
info@proislepublishing.com

PROISLE PUBLISHING

TABLE OF CONTENTS

FOREWORD — XI
ACKNOWLEDGMENTS — XV
DEDICATION — XVII
PREFACE — 19

    About Leader As Servant Leadership (LSL) Model — 22
    About the Authentic Leader as Servant (ALS) — 25
    About the ALS Courses — 26

CHAPTER 1
    UNDERSTANDING LEADERSHIP ATTRIBUTES — 35

    Functional Definitions — 35
    Comparisons With Other Works — 40
    Principle of Leadership Attribute — 42
    Authentic Leadership Attributes — 43
    Summary 1 Understanding Leadership Process — 49

CHAPTER 2
    LEADERSHIP DISCIPLESHIP LEADERSHIP ATTRIBUTE — 53

    Characteristics of Discipleship Attribute — 54
    Principle of Discipline Attribute — 56
    Summary 2 Leadership Discipleship Leadership Attribute — 57

CHAPTER 3
    DEVELOPING THE ACTS OF AFFECTIVE-LOVE — 61

    Summary 3 Developing the Acts of Personal Discipline Instruction — 64

CHAPTER 4
    DEVELOPING THE ACTS OF INTENTIONAL DISCIPLESHIP — 67

    Strategies for Intentional Discipleship — 67
    Summary 4 Developing the Acts of International Discipleship — 69

CHAPTER 5
    DEVELOPING THE ACTS OF ATTENTIVE DISCIPLESHIP — 73

    Summary 5 Developing the Acts of Attentive Discipleship — 78

CHAPTER 6
    DEVELOPING THE ACTS OF REPRODUCTIVE DISCIPLESHIP — 83

    Strategies to Commission Disciples — 86

ALS DISCIPLESHIP LEADERSHIP
ATTRIBUTES, PRINCIPLES, & PRACTICES

Summary 6 Developing the Acts of Reproductive Discipleship-------------- 89

TOPIC INDEX   93
REFERENCES   95

FOREWORD

The modern world today is obsessed with standardization and modalities. As a result, in the realm of leadership, many books have spout associated leadership theories and models and explain them as the path to follow. However, the critical dimensions that distinguish the effectiveness of any leadership process are the values and attribute the leader brings to the table; desired change is influenced by leadership styles or standards. These many standards and theories of leadership often are not in step with the changing times or the followers' needs. The trend is a bit like stocking different kinds of foods in a grocery store and expecting that they will meet everybody's needs the same way and at all times. Aisles are packed with varieties of food with expiration dates in the future, but getting the best deal on the products is what really matters to those who buy and use the products

In many ways, this is the state of leadership in the modern world. Increasingly, even leaders of public institutions are tasked with turning a profit for themselves or the organization they serve. The idea of a "leader" seems to float uneasily alongside the ranks of fundraisers or profit raisers in contrast to any kind of role model for followers or employees. That which is knowable, measurable, and marketable has surpassed the difficult intangibility of strong moral leadership attributes as the central guideline for achievement and success.

In this complicated space, Dr. Sylvanus Wosu introduces his complex idea of the Leader as a Servant Leadership, which is in this book, modeled on Christian tradition. Like all intricate ideas, Dr. Wosu's central point depends on a paradox: a person is best qualified to lead when he or she is most ready to serve. This paradox has been monopolized rhetorically by "public servants" who often serve either self-interest or the interests of specific lobbies. The Authentic Leader as Servant penetrates past the superficial concept of "serving" and details the internal state of true servitude or Servanthood.

While the book is primarily focused on the Christian model of leadership attributes such as discipleship, empathy, affection, and Servanthood, it does so not merely on the grounds of blind faith, but rather via numerous contemporary sociological and business-driven studies on how leaders should seek a leader-follower relationship that is simultaneously productive and nurturing. Dr. Wosu's most piercing insights always involve this secular–Christian dialogue. This book demonstrates that Christ's model for leadership is one that may exist successfully outside the confines of a faith relationship; it places the values of Christ's religious significance in leadership at the center of the framework. It is clear from Dr. Wosu's generous own life story of faith—a faith tested by humbling difficulties—is at the center of both his orientation and motivation for writing.

In language that is so concise, it is often illustrated in mathematical formulas; Dr. Wosu explains the deep structural integrity of Christ's Leader as the Servant Leadership model. One could imagine leaders of any doctrine benefiting from the analyses contained in these pages. The book's message repeatedly encourages the reader to imagine a scenario or reflect on memories and personal experiences to prove or test its many points. Thus, the book depends on a form of praxis, a lesson that could be or has been enacted, by the participating reader. I am very impressed at the volume and level of thinking of the author. Parts of the book involve his personal story, which is especially riveting. I cannot imagine what he had to endure, which he referred to as a" wilderness walk," to accomplish the goal he set for himself. His life stories on these pages are inspiring and stimulating.

In this way, the text eschews dogmatism in favor of the self-discovery Socratic Method of teaching and learning. The reader is not badgered into complying with a religious objective but is rather asked to consider the applicability of difficult biblical concepts in relation to modern life. It is a fascinating and very thought-provoking read.

Hence, the book does not seek to make the leader a servant, a cookie-cutter corporate buzzword, but rather asks the reader to imagine him or herself interacting with a range of concepts. One of Dr. Wosu's great strengths is his reservation when it comes to forcing his reading's interpretation on the material he presents.

The book parallels Biblical and modern leadership scenarios in ways that consistently provoke thought, and while it is clear Dr. Wosu has his particular leadership style; the space for the reader's own thoughts is always left open.

The book could not have been written in any other way with integrity. Its format and formulas are offered to the reader of the leader as a servant role that it analyzes in its pages. To find a text that instructs from this humble position is profoundly refreshing in a genre that is often packaged inside a cover with a sizeable picture of the "modest" author, smiling egotistically beneath a name spelled out in large, gold lettering. Throughout its pages, this text feels as if it serves the reader.

In the end, this is the most satisfying aspect of the book. There is no standardized approach to achieving successful leadership. There is no promise of power and a bigger payday; in fact, the book often proffers just the opposite. The reader is not encouraged to devalue the experience of leadership by finding some economic metric for marking success but is rather asked to think deeply about the most basic elements of internal and social interaction within the framework of a Christian tradition. What this means will be different for every reader. Indeed, even in the context of single chapters, I found myself questioning or re-evaluating moments of my own life. This book serves; it doesn't feel like filling in multiple-choice questions, staring at a wall of flavorless grocery products, or hearing the endless servant promises of today's political scene. It feels like a humble invitation to consider a single paradoxical element of a profoundly productive tradition.

-Tobias Bates

Acknowledgments

A book on leadership attributes as aspects of Servant Leadership sprouted from the wealth of knowledge and the inspirations of many other leaders. Their writings were sources of inspiration, challenges, and examples of excellence to emulate.

Dr. Enefaa N. Wosu, my wife and life partner, for her love, commitment, and prayer support, especially during those long night hours I was not there for her and her constant reminder of who I must be as a leader-servant. Without her support, forbearance, wisdom, and encouragement, this project would not have been completed; I say, thank you very much.

And to God alone be all the glory and honor for the divine inspiration and guidance in initiating and completing this life-transforming book project.

DEDICATION

I humbly submit this book back unto the gracious hands of God who inspired the writings through His Holy Spirit!

I dedicate this book to my virtuous wife of 45 years, Rev. (Dr.) Enefaa Wosu whose spiritual leadership is an important gateway to our home, and to our four wonderful children—Prof. Eliada Wosu-Griffin EL, HeCareth, Tamuno-Emi, and Chidinma. From them all, I learnt what it meant to be a leader-servant. I could not be blessed with better teachers.

PREFACE

What characteristics did Biblical leaders like the Apostle Paul, Moses, Joshua, and Nehemiah as servants of their people display outwardly that distinguished them from other leaders, both then and now? The Apostle Paul kept his focus to *emulate* Christ and endured all the infirmities and persecutions he suffered to complete his goal to preach the gospel of Jesus Christ. He inspired Timothy and others through his effective *discipleship* leadership to imitate him as he emulated Christ. Moses' outward display of his *trust* in God's power earned him a good level of trust from the people and empowered him for the mission of delivery of God's children from bondage in Egypt; he had to *reproduce* himself in Joshua to complete the mission. But the greatest of them was Jesus Christ, who humbly sacrificed His life to finish the work of redemption. In His *Servanthood*, commitment, and love for the people, He became the ultimate *model* of a leader as a servant to *emulate*.

Let's consider for a moment secular leaders in these current times! For example, think of Henry Ford, who founded the successful Ford Motor Company; Bill Gates who created the global empire that is Microsoft; Albert Einstein, who in many ways is synonymous with a genius for his contributions to modern physics; Abraham Lincoln, remembered as one of the greatest presidents and leaders of United States; and many others like these we cannot mention. What did all these leaders have in common? What propelled them to turn their initial failures or challenges into eventual successes? None had a direct mentor or inherited any fortune from their parents. Nevertheless, they all eventually succeeded. These people can be distinguished from others based on their self-will to succeed, their self-confidence and belief in themselves, their self-determination, and their perseverance, among other characteristics. The distinguishing characteristics displayed externally in service or relationships toward others are the outward functional attributes that define that leader.

Think about yourself as a student, faculty member, or that new executive. What was it that made your journey to success different and even great? Students and colleagues, when they see or hear about my display of what I have referred to as the 'wilderness walk of faith', have asked me to share the critical attitudinal elements that made me remain inwardly resilient and undaunted and yet outwardly joyful in the difficulties I had faced. This book is the result of those reflections. Let me explain one such teaching moment.

Many years ago, sitting in my research lab on a Saturday morning trying to finish writing my dissertation, a fellow graduate student walked into the room to talk with me. He was contemplating terminating his graduate studies. He was a privileged single male student but felt the load was just too much.

"Sylvanus," he asked, with seriousness in his eyes, "your research advisor suggested that I should ask you, 'what is it that makes you tick?'.'What is it about you that makes you joyful and at peace with yourself and determined to finish, no matter the situations and high expectations we face in this department?"

What he asked me were deeply reflective questions, but I was willing and excited to answer them. Even so, before I do, let's look at the context. At that period in my life, I had four little children as a graduate student; in fact, more children than any of the faculties at that time, except for one faculty member who had eight children. I received little or no support from the department. I was then an international alien, did not qualify for financial aid, and was not given any research assistant position. I was, therefore, self-supported with two off-campus part-time jobs. I joked at being a minority of minorities, the only student in the department with such a label,—but I was self-willed to succeed. My adaptability attribute, coupled with perseverance and resilience, was all that I needed to succeed despite the odds against me. In every exam, homework assignment, or project I had to compete with students with full financial aid, plus they had nothing to distract their attention from their studies. I lived with the attitude that using disadvantages as an excuse was not an option. Aspiring to earn my Ph.D. was a life dream, and I was willing to give my ultimate best to actualize that dream even in the face of challenges. The choice was mine!

So I looked at my classmate and all I could see was a student striding through a valley through which I also walked. He needed me to show him how to walk the walk, to empathize with him. To answer his question, I smiled, not that I wanted to, but because it was just who

I was. The joy he attributed to me was an overflow of my appreciation of God's grace that His life in me was externally manifesting His light to bless someone else. It was a great teaching moment; I capitalized on it to tell my classmate that my joy was not about me. He could see physically but about He who was in me, he could not see in the flesh; I needed him to know that I was just showing forth His life in me. At first, my classmate did not understand the spiritual prose or metaphor I was using. He looked surprised but open to hearing more.

I did not ask if he was a Christian. However, right on my desk was my small green pocket Bible. I opened to 2 Corinthians 12:9 (NIV) and handed it to him to read. As he read the passage: "But he said to me, 'My grace is sufficient for you, for my power is made perfect in weakness.' Therefore, I will boast all the more gladly about my weaknesses, so that Christ's power may rest on me," I noticed how absorbed he was in the words

He looked astonished and read it again, this time silently. "This is interesting, but what does this mean?" He asked. I took his question to mean, "How does this relate to my question?

I explained to my friend that the external attitudes he or my advisors saw in me that warranted the question, "What makes you tick" were inspired by my inner value system based on my faith in this same Christ and His teachings. My desire to manifest His life and self-confidence is all because of what He has promised in His word if I believed. I have believed His words and have gained self-determination and faith to make the right choices through Him for my life, and his spirit has given me perseverance and resilience to focus on finishing strong in pursuit of any goal. "With that faith, I have continued, more passionately and excitedly; I can look at my challenges and vulnerabilities and delight joyfully in them, even as an alien minority of minorities! His grace and power have empowered me to do all things I want to do. That is what makes me tick," I explained.

He looked at me as if he got his answer. "Wow, thanks!" he said, looking inspired and ready to face his challenges. As we concluded with a prayer, and he stood up to leave, I pointed empathetically to his face and said, "If I made it despite my challenges, you have absolutely no excuse but to persevere to complete your studies; you can make it too!"

It is fitting to report that this encounter with my classmate transformed his will and determination to continue. Yes, he was encouraged and went on to complete his graduate studies. He emulated self-will and perseverance from the example of the most vulnerable of all students in the department.

The inner value system of a Leader-Servant is founded not only on his faith but his self-will, coupled with self-leadership; it is the greatest mentor who can turn any situation into an inconceivable success. Self-will is the primary driver for determination, resilience, and perseverance. It is what wakes you up in the morning to ask for strength to do whatever it is you are setting out to do. Based on my life walk of faith, I can state with absolute certainty that faith is the unseen assuredness that can empower you to turn your life's probable impossibilities into great and improbable possibilities.

ABOUT LEADER AS SERVANT LEADERSHIP (LSL) MODEL

Looking at the testimony above, do you know the source that energizes the characteristics you display outside and how your inner self is related to what others see outside? What distinguishes you from others is what combines to define your attributes! As a follower, can you identify the characteristics that distinguish your leaders? As an executive, how do you base your evaluation of yourself? Or how do you evaluate that brand-new manager or new youth director you want to hire? To what do you compare the individual's qualities when you look at his CV? What is the basis of your measure? Do you know if you are a substantial leader? These personal questions and much more are the subjects of this two-volume book, 'The Authentic Leader as Servant Part I: The Outward Leadership Attributes, Principles, and Practices', is written in two parts; the second part 'The Leader as Servant Leadership Model. Part II'; deals with the Inner Strength Leadership Attributes, Principles, and Practices.

When we think about today's corporate greed, deepening divide between the haves and have-not, gridlock in political systems, conflicts and wars, high divorce rates, and the rich young ruler in the Bible, it is easy to agree that all these people share a few things in common: self-centeredness, pride, lack of compassion, and greed. There is a great need in today's suffering world for leader-servants who display leadership attributes. These attributes should be oriented toward selfless service to others. Indeed, our world is increasingly drifting away from global serving reality toward the self and apathy. The most credible message or model for a possible solution to this dilemma and the answer to several complex leadership questions can be found in the foundation of the ultimate leader-servant, Jesus Christ. This book defines the Leader as Servant Leadership attribute as the combined acts of two or more distinctive functional leadership characteristics exhibited in service and relationship toward others. There is no better time than now for a book that presents comprehensive and irrevocable facts and principles regarding how to develop effective attributes of the leader-servant.

The Leader as Servant Leadership Model

My first book on this subject, The Leader as Servant Leadership Model, explains that Jesus' servant leadership model is based on the notion of a Leader as a Servant and not on a Servant as Leader. There are four distinct differences between a Servant as Leader (Servant-leader) and the Leader as Servant (leader--servant) models. It is pertinent to highlight them here to connect to this book, Authentic Leader as Servant.

A Leader as Servant is a leader first. The leader–servant as a leader does not in the line of duty go projecting or lording his or her power and authority over others but is the person to lead the process of influencing desired changes in others through his humble example of being a servant or having a serviceable attitude toward others. He or she is a serving leader, not a lording leader. He leads as a servant by putting others' needs above his own needs and rights. Jesus emphasized the word "as" meaning that the leader (the Master) chooses to serve as a servant even though he is the leader. A leader–servant emulates Jesus, who gave up all rights, and emptied and expended Himself on His followers. He empowered them to become more like Him. A leader-servant is known as a leader first but is seen as a great leader by his humble attendant heart and acts of service to others. His greatness comes from his ability to put others above himself.

Leader as Servant is a Biblical Concept. The model or image of a humble serving leader motivated Jesus' disciples to see that if their master could do this for them, they must also be able to do it for others. Jesus clearly demonstrated the process of leader-as-servant leadership. In some cases, He chose to serve by leading when He wanted to create the image or model of the leader-servant in certain acts. In other cases, He chose to lead by serving, when he showed care and empathy toward the people and led the disciples to see empathy as a leadership attribute.

Leader as Servant is an Authentic Leadership Model to follow. The Leader as the Servant leadership model intentionally positions Jesus as an original model of a leader to follow.

He was serving His disciples to demonstrate that the process of becoming a great leader was earned through humble acts of service to others; He made them understand that He was empowering them to succeed Him as leader-servants through service to others. The result was an incomparable legacy of leadership that changed their communities. The fact that Jesus relinquished his rights or shared His power did not diminish His power and influence. In fact, his influence increased at least 11 X 100%, if we ignore the one case of Judas.

The Leader as Servant Transforms Organizational Culture. The proposed LSL model seeks to transform and sustain the community or organization by instilling key leadership values or "leadership presence" among followers or an organization's members. Change is sustained when everyone in the organization takes ownership of the change. Rather than focusing on leading more followers to be great followers who conform to the organizational culture, LSL seeks to lead and empower better leaders to be distinguished leaders and community builders.

There are four distinctions, which clearly differentiate many of the existing servants as Leader-based philosophies in relation to servant leadership from my LSL model. Even in the corporate or institutional worlds, there is nothing better than Jesus on which to base Servant Leadership. There is nothing more authentic and impacting than the servant leadership modeled by the life and teachings of Jesus Christ.

The LSL model uses exploratory questions, scenarios, and graphic visualizations to excite critical thinking in ways no other book on this subject has yet attempted. Several personal testimonies of my wilderness walk of faith with God are used to connect the reader to real-life experiences of the concepts discussed. The riveting effect is that the text engages and encourages the reader to walk through the experiences presented. The aim is to inspire the reader spiritually, mentally, and professionally with this far-reaching exposition on the subject of servant leadership.

ABOUT THE AUTHENTIC LEADER AS SERVANT (ALS)

The *Authentic Leader as Servant* argues that no leadership model is as authentic, other-centered, able to build communities, and productive and service-oriented as the model of our ultimate leader-servant, Jesus Christ. No source can provide a better point of reference than that provided in the Bible. Hence, this book aims to be more than just a text on leadership; it hopes to be a personal discovery for those who aspire to develop effective leadership attributes that grow leaders as servants who ultimately develop thriving other-centered communities. This book presents a comprehensive, biblically-based study regarding how to develop these attributes and how they are applied in a servant leadership process. In this biblical context and for clarity, Servant Leadership means *Leader-as-Servant Leadership*. A *leader-servant* refers to a *leader as a servant*, which is distinct from a servant-leader or servant as leader.

Leader as Servant Leadership attributes are shaped by the Leadership's Inner Value system, which consists of character, motivation, and commitment. The *Authentic Leader as Servant* is presented as a necessary resource to complement my *The Leader as Servant Leadership (LSL) Model*. The LSL model integrates a transformative leadership framework and interactive dimensions of Servant Leadership. Leader as Servant Leadership is a process in which a leader, in his leadership position, purposefully chooses to put others' rights and needs above his positional rights and personal needs. He then serves, enables, and empowers followers for growth that builds a thriving organization. The LSL model looks at the predominant Servant Leadership concepts and shares how they compare with biblical principles on how we should lead and be led.

ABOUT THE ALS COURSES

The three books, *LSL Model* and *The Authentic Leader as Servant* (Parts I and II), together demonstrate that with today's global visions to reach people of all races and cultures, now is the time for an authentic servant's heart of service. Those visions and the leadership processes are most effective with the appropriate leadership attributes centered more on people than on the organization, principles regarding how to develop effective attributes of leader-servant.

The ALS I and II combined presented twenty leaders as servant leadership attributes. The series of ALS courses supply training guide to understand, develop, and practice the attributes in a leadership process. Each course is independent and self-contained and does not depend on completing any other course in the series of 20 courses. It is, however strongly recommended, in fact a must read, that chapters 1 and 2 in each series be covered as they lay the foundation of LSL model on which ALS is based.

ALS (Parts I & II) Course Layout

The *Authentic Leader as Servant (ALS)* leadership (parts I and II) book has been broken down into 20 courses in workbook format to achieve three goals 1) Self-discovery of the acts of developing the attribute under review in the course, 2) deeper understanding of the principles, research and biblical teaching behind the attributes, and 3) Learning the strategies for practicing the attributes.

Instruction

The set of questions following each chapter are designed to serve as a guide to discover, explore, and practice the essential ALS leadership attributes, principles, and practices in leadership process. The questions are comprehensive review based on the content of this specific chapter only.

To maximize the learning outcomes, the learner must read through this chapter and sections. Some referenced scriptures in the book are repeated in the summaries for added review if needed, even though they were discussed in the section in which they apply.

> The exercises that follow each chapter will help you in not only understanding your own strength and weaknesses in your acts of the attribute but will guide you in developing practical strategies you can apply in self-leadership process or helping others grow in leadership
>
> All answers to the questions are contained in the associated chapter or sections; consultation of new sources, except for the reference scriptures, is not needed. Thus, it is expected that you answer the questions after you have read the associated section or chapter of the workbook. The scripture or other references cited are only for references as they already discussed in the book

---

ALS I Course 1: Affection Leadership Attribute—*Affection flows from a person to produce positive emotions for the well-being of another person.*

An average person will define the word "love" in the sense that affection is a characteristic of love. Nevertheless, that definition clouds the functional meaning of affection as an attribute of a leader-servant. Affection is a love action intentionally given to someone to create favorable emotion. We experience a positive emotion when we receive or give affection. In his acts of affection, the Apostle Paul communicated to the Corinthian Christians how he spoke to them freely with an open heart, because it was an important way to give affection (2 Corinthians 6:11-13). He also spoke of longing for them with the affection of Jesus Christ (Philippians 1:8); an affection that needs to be mutual (1 Peter 1:7). How is the affection leadership attribute an outward leadership attribute? This course explores this and other questions to discover the characteristics of affection attributes and to formulate a functional principle based on the expected outcome of affection and the effective use of these attributes in leadership.

ALS I Course 2: Discipleship Leadership Attribute- *Discipleship transforms and empowers followers for service leadership that grows communities.*

Discipleship as an act of developing a follower toward a specific goal is an important function of leadership to equip others to lead. *Discipleship transforms and empowers followers for service leadership that grows communities.* A disciple is a follower who willingly chooses to follow the master and submits to his discipleship and authority. In that regard, Jesus wanted all his followers to be his disciples and ambassadors because a disciple is always a follower. Organizationally, a follower could be a junior employee, any employee in a brand-new department, a new younger faculty, or just any person that needs to be guided through a journey of professional growth and good success. This course focuses on the general growth of followers through the acts of discipleship and presents the critical characteristics of discipleship as a leadership outward attribute. Functional definitions of leadership discipleship attributes and its principle will be presented based on those characteristics. Each characteristic will be discussed in detail with emphasis on strategies of how they can be further developed or practiced as a part of the servant leadership process.

ALS I Course 3: Emulation Leadership Attribute—*A great leader-servant outwardly and positively inspires a pattern of good works for others to follow.*

To emulate is to strive to be like someone else or to follow someone else's example by imitating something that inspires you about that person. This course evaluates how to learn from someone good leadership qualities to develop yours. How did you use what you learned from following the footstep of your hero to grow your leadership qualities. Jesus in the scripture modeled humility and Servanthood he wanted his disciples to develop same qualities. Emulation as a leadership attribute shares some characteristics with transformative leadership, where a leader intentionally conveys a clear vision of a goal, inspires the passion for the work toward the goal, and motivates the followers to follow. As a leader, how do you model a characteristic behavior for someone to follow or develop? How is Leadership Emulation Leadership Attribute an outward leadership attribute? This course explores this and other questions to discover the characteristics of affection attributes and to formulate a functional principle based on the expected outcome of effective use of these attributes in leadership.

ALS I Course 4: Generosity Leadership Attribute: *Generosity is an outward measure of the level of sacrifice, what is shared, or the impact a giving makes, not just the size of the giving*

Generosity can be defined as "the *habit of giving* without expecting anything in return. It can involve offering time, assets, or talents to aid someone in need." Such habits can include spending your personal money, time, and/or labor for the welfare of others or expending (suffering or being consumed or spending) for others' well-being. When political leaders or Board members 'vote their conscience' on important issues that affect others, what is that "conscience" and how do such leaders contribute to the welfare of others? How can you, "Do all you can, with what you have, in the time you have, in the place where you are" for the betterment of humanity   All giving to help humanity is crucial to help meet the needs of the most vulnerable of God's children, as demonstrated by God as attribute of God, In this course, we will explore what distinguishes a leader's act of giving from his inside intentions. The key leadership characteristics of generosity will be discussed with respect to Servant-Leadership generosity Attributes and Principles and the details how a leader-servant can develop those characteristics and then effectively practice service leadership.

ALS I Course 5: Healing-Care Leadership Attribute: *Comforting others in any trouble with the comfort with which God comforts us, brings healing-wholeness*

What is healing Care and what does it mean in practical terms to you as a leader? Effective leadership begins with an emotionally and spiritually healthy leader who can reconcile and bring comfort to the followers, irrespective of followers' feelings (good or bad) toward the leader. The healing attribute and personal security complement each other. You must have the capacity for self-healing and individual security if you are to meet others' comforts. Personal security provides the infrastructure to support leaders in adversity and heal others that are hurting. A leader's or a group's success is measured by the strength of the weakest member or follower in the group or team… Healing is one of the most abstract and least understood attributes in leadership, and yet one of the most important. The key distinguishing characteristics will be explored to formulate a working definition and principle of leadership healing-care attributes based on those characteristics. Each characteristic will be discussed in detail with emphasis on strategies of how they can be further developed or practiced by a leader-servant as part of the servant leadership process.

ALS I Course 6: Influence Leadership Attribute-*The true measure of leadership success in affecting desired change in conduct, performance, and relational connections in others is influence*

Leadership is an integrative process in which a person applies appropriate (leadership) attributes to guide and influence the desired attitudinal changes in others toward accomplishing a particular goal. Eight five percent of CEOs of top companies surveyed on their climb to leadership ladder said they were "influenced by another leader," compared to 10% and 5% for "natural gifting" and "result of a crisis," respectively. When we consider influence as a servant leadership attribute, we are talking about a distinguishing leadership characteristic that displays on the outside what a leader is inside, influence takes on a deeper meaning. In this course, the key leadership characteristics of influence will be identified and explored from research to frame definitions of the Servant-Leadership influence attribute and principle. Based on those characteristics, the key outcomes of effective leadership influence l how a leader-servant can develop those characteristics and then effectively practice service leadership.

ALS I Course 7: Persuasion Leadership Attribute—*The means of transforming others to a new perspective is through empathetic persuasion.*

Persuasion attribute affords the leader the capacity to convince his followers or others to believe and engage in a new idea or goal through encouragement rather than using his positional authority or intimidation. Because members of the group may already have their views on an issue, the leader must carefully approach persuasion as a learning process to avoid conflicts or polarizing the group. He must unify the diversity of views to get buy-in and willingness to agree and follow. The leader-servant primarily relies on making decisions within an organization based on persuasion rather than positional authority. In other words, you will never hear the Leader-servant say, "Do it because I am the boss, and I say to." This particular element offers one of the clearest distinctions between the traditional authoritarian model of leadership and the concept of Servant leadership. In this course, we will explore the technique of convincing rather than coercing as one of the most effective ways a leader-servant can build consensus within groups. Key characteristics of persuasion leadership attribute will be found, fully discussed, and modeled from the examples in the lives of other leaders.

ALS I Course 8: Responsibility Leadership Attribute—*Great leaders produce successors for legacy and greater courses as an expected product of an effective leadership reproduction.*

In his book, *360 Degree Leader*, John C. Maxwell says, "Great leaders don't use people so they can win. They lead people so they can all lead together." Such great leaders, like Jesus, Moses, Paul, and others developed other leaders through a process of reproduction. Is it possible for leaders of today to reproduce their vision in others so that can lead and build a legacy together? The answer to this question is of course yes. However, the effectiveness of a leader duplicating his leadership qualities in a follower depends on the leadership reproduction attribute of the leader. This course explores the distinguishing characteristics of reproduction as an outward attribute in servant leadership. Functional definitions of leadership reproduction attribute and its principle will be presented based on those characteristics. Each characteristic of reproduction attributes will be discussed in detail with emphasis on strategies of how they can be further developed or practiced by a leader-servant as part of the servant leadership process.

ALS I Course 9: Servanthood Leadership Attribute— *A leader-servant is most qualified to lead when ready to serve as a servant for the growth of others.*

The last time you engaged in a practical act of service on the job, at home, church, or in your community, what were the key elements in that act of service? Did you serve because you wanted to and chose to serve? Or was it because someone asked you to? The ultimate goal is for the leader's life to positively transform many lives in his or her community of followers. Consider the New Testament teachings of Jesus, who demonstrated the ultimate Leader as Servant Leadership. Jesus equated greatness to serving unpretentiously (humbly, as would a child), and He equated leading with choosing to serve others. That is the first affirmative test of authenticity for this attribute. What were the distinguishing characteristics that enabled you to serve? How is the Leadership Servanthood an outward leadership attribute? This course will give answers and meanings to these and personal reflective questions to discover the distinguishing characteristics of The Leadership Servanthood attribute. Functional definitions of The Leadership Servanthood attribute and principle will be provided based on the identified characteristics. Readers will benefit from numerous techniques, personal examples, empirical case study, and applications of the concepts.

ALS I Course 10: Trust-Integrity Leadership Attribute—*True leadership trust produces assured trustee's confidence and readiness to follow based on the credibility, competence, and shared relational connections of the trusted.*

A study examined more than 75 key components of employee satisfaction in top leadership and found that trust and confidence was the single most reliable predictor of employee satisfaction in an organization. This course will examine the results of the above study with respect to servant leadership, and how a leader-servant increases the satisfaction of the followers in an organization. When the organization is going through some challenges, how can a leader be credible in helping the followers understand the company's mission and strategy? How can he share information on how the company or institution, or department is doing and how the followers or employees will be affected? Suppose the organization's strategy is not aligned with its inner value or character, how does the leader build trust in followers or earn trust from them? Organizational leadership trust has been defined by as "an employee's willingness to take a risk for a leader with the expectation that, in exchange, the leader will behave in some desired way." The course will examine how the element of reliance and confidence in the actions of the trusted and organization are characterized by a combination of Competence (Can they do the job?), Benevolence (Do they care about me?), and Integrity (Are they honest?).

Referenced Scriptures

A variety of Bible translations from over 11,200 original Hebrew, Aramaic, and Greek words to about 6,000 English words do exist with variations in meanings and emphases. I am not a biblical scholar and do not pretend to be one; Hence, I have avoided researching the roots of these words and personally prefer New King James Version (NKJV). I have intentionally used other translations for three main reasons; first, to allow for increased impact and alignment of words to the most desired meaning and emphasis in the concepts being addressed. Second, I wanted new and personal discovery of meanings from translations with which I have not been familiar. And third, I wanted to allow readers who may desire translations other than the NKJV the benefit of their preferred translations. Hence, in addition to the NKJV, other translations used in the book include New International Version (NIV), New Living Translation (NLT), King James Version (KJV), English Standard Version (ESV), and Good News Translation (GNT). Unless otherwise specified, NKJV should be assumed.

Sylvanus Nwakanma Wosu

CHAPTER 1
UNDERSTANDING LEADERSHIP ATTRIBUTES

Leadership attribute is the combined acts of two or more distinctive functional leadership characteristics exhibited in service and relationship toward others.

The starting point of our discussion is the understanding of the key functional definitions and concepts that describe the theme of this book. In general, 1 will define leadership as an integrative process in which a person applies appropriate attributes to guide and influence the sought-after attitudinal changes in others toward accomplishing a particular goal. Specifically, the Leader as Servant Leadership is a process in which a leader intentionally chooses to put the follower's rights and needs above his positional rights and personal needs, and serves, enables, and empowers them for desired spiritual and professional growth that builds thriving communities.

FUNCTIONAL DEFINITIONS

In the context of these definitions, I will begin the descriptions of the leadership attributes of an authentic leader-servant by offering a functional definition of Leadership Attributes, and showing how that definition differs from those of Leadership Character, Characteristics, and Traits.

Leadership Character is the sum total of personal qualities in leadership, such as honesty, values, vision, trust, and so on that make up the moral capital of the leader; Leadership character should describe who the leader is inside or the leader's basic personality traits.

The Leadership Characteristics describe the distinctive characteristics or features of a leader, such as attitudes, competencies, skills, and specific experiences that go beyond his character (personality). Leadership characteristics determine how (through skills and competencies) the leader leads or take actions in the process of leadership in any particular situation;

The Leadership traits are the distinguishing leadership characteristics of a leader (these are things that define his leadership characteristics), which differentiate from personality traits... Leadership traits are the set of characteristics that define a particular leader's leadership. This means that a leadership characteristic is a trait when it is a unique characteristic of the leader.

Leadership Attributes, unlike leadership character, characteristics, and traits, is *a leadership attribute and the combined act of two or more distinctive functional leadership characteristics exhibited in service and relationship toward others* or traits externally displayed in action toward others. All leadership attributes grow out of the leadership inner value system but can be externally displayed predominantly as an outbound or outward attribute or both:

1. **Outbound Attributes:** These are distinctive outward-bound attributes emanating from the inner strength of the leader to support external conduct in service and relationships toward others. They form the internal core functional qualities that motivate or enhance the outward manifestation of the inside character toward others. The outbound attribute such as listening and vision, for example, are the direct results of the inner values of the leader such as patience, hearing, love, humility, or all the fruits of the spirit.
2. **Outward Attributes:** These are distinctive functional outward outer visible attributes emanating from the richness of the outbound and inner values of the leader. For example, external attributes such as Servanthood, emulation/modeling, empathy, etc. are outflows from the leader who will directly impact the follower. Outward attributes can be enriched by the outbound (inner) attributes. As shown in Figure 1, the outward attributes in general form the outer core of

functional attributes in the leader as servant leadership, but they can share some overlapping functions with the outbound attributes.

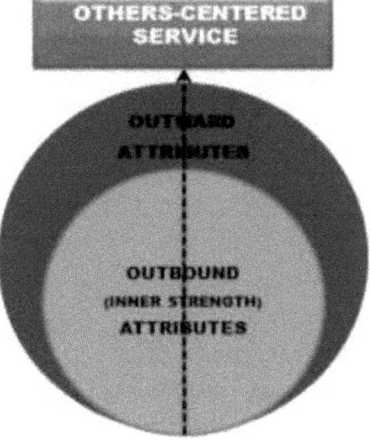

Figure 1.1. Servant leadership functional attributes

In summary, a leadership attribute is more than an ability or a characteristic; it is making those characteristics or abilities functional as part of how the leader acts (his habits) in service to others and applying those characteristics (beyond just having them) in personal and service relations to others. The character or known characteristic defines some aspects of your abilities or who you are inside— e.g. honest, humble, brave, etc. Your attribute, on the other hand, defines your habits; a display of how you use your characteristics, or the actions you exhibit toward others because of who you are inside. For example, empathy as a leadership characteristic becomes a leadership attribute if the followers can distinguish the leader's acts or habits of empathy, such as walking through with his followers in their state of suffering to bring wholeness; otherwise, it is just a characteristic or ability. Leadership attributes toward others are what impact the followers' and the organizational growth more than ability and competence.

In addressing one of the self-righteous hypocritical attributes of servitude leadership, Jesus called leader-servants to be "inside-out" leaders that reflect credibility; indeed, leaders should not appear outwardly righteous when they are full of hypocrisy and lawlessness in their hearts. He was describing "inside–out" as an authentic leadership attribute measured by the display of credibility a leadership attribute!

The measuring stick of a leader-servant is Jesus Christ. We measure ourselves unto the measure of the status of the fullness of Christ (Ephesians 4:13).

The leadership attributes of an authentic leader as a servant are encapsulated in **SERVANT/SERVING LEADERSHIP** are listed in Table 1.1, and defined in Table 1.2: *Servanthood, Emulation, Responsibility, Vision, Navigation, Adaptability, Trust, Listening, Empathy, Affection, Discipleship, Encouragement, Reproduction, Stewardship, Healing-Care, Initiation, Integrity,* and *Persuasion*. Other support attributes include *Influence, Courage, and Generosity*.

The attributes have been separated into Outward and Outbound (Inner Strength) leadership Attributes. As shown in Table 1.1, each of these attributes has three or more leadership characteristics. As such, more than 65 leadership characteristics are covered in these 20 attributes. For example, a leader's Servanthood leadership attribute is characterized by his willing servant's heart of selfless role humility, sacrifice, and submissiveness. The more these are present in a leader, the more effective the servant leadership.

Table 1.1: The functional leader-servant leadership Outbound (Inner Strength) and Outward attributes

	LEADER-SERVANT LEADERSHIP ATTRIBUTES			INNER STRENGTH ATTRIBUTES	OUTWARD ATTRIBUTES
S	Servanthood	L	Listening	Adaptability	Affection
E	Emulation	E	Empathy	Courage	Discipleship
R	Responsibility	A	Affection	Empathy	Emulation
V	Vision	D	Discipleship	Encouragement	Generosity
A	Adaptability	E	Encouragement	Initiation	Healing–Care
N	Navigation	R	Reproduction	Listening	Influence
T	Trust	S	Stewardship	Navigation	Persuasion
I	Influence	H	Healing–Care	Responsibility	Reproduction
G	Generosity	I	Initiation	Stewardship	Servanthood
C	Courage	P	Persuasion	Vision	Trust/Integrity

The list does not assume that a leader has to be excellent in all attributes or even have all of them to be an effective Leader–Servant. However, the more of these attributes the leader displays in his acts of service toward others, the more productive he or she will be, and the further his impact on the followers and organization. The table also shows that two or more attributes can share common characteristics, which can be applied or observed in different contexts. For example, a leader's ability to inspire followers can be seen in his acts of discipleship, empowerment, an.d encouragement attributes in the context in which these attributes apply. Each attribute is exhibited either as a part of the outbound inner strength attribute of a leader or a part of the outward attribute. Table 1.1 is not an exhaustive list of attributes; in fact, there are hundreds of such attributes. This is just the starting point.

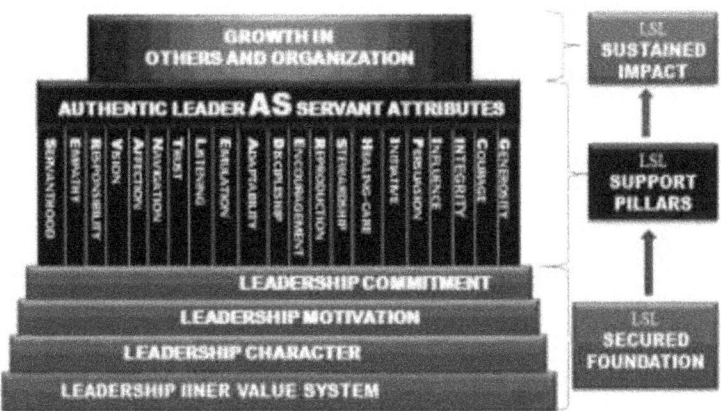

Figure 1.2: Servant leadership outward attributes (dark blue) and relationship to four foundational layers of the LSL Model

Figure 1.2 shows that the leader's attributes are shaped and secured by his four foundational layers (leadership inner value system, leadership character, motivation, and commitment). The attributes of the leader–servants are also conceptualized as the support pillars that will establish and support the personal authenticity of the leader, what the leader, does and the effectiveness of the leadership process. Thus, the attributes represent functional pillars of authentic leadership that can be learned or enriched as described in detail in the subsequent chapters. The combined effect of a secured foundation and stable support pillars will make a sustained impact on the growth of followers and the organization.

COMPARISONS WITH OTHER WORKS

The original works by Greenleaf (1970) in servant leadership [1] have been reviewed by Larry Spears (1996), who identified listening, empathy, healing, awareness, persuasion, conceptualization, foresight, stewardship, commitment to the growth of others, and building community as the ten distinguishing characteristics of servant leadership. [2] Russell (2001) has studied these attributes and have shown them to be essential in servant leadership and concluded that these qualities generally "grow out of the inner values and beliefs of individual leaders." [3] Russell and Stone (2002) extended the Greenleaf 10 attributes to 20 attributes observed in servant-leaders. These 20 attributes were categorized by these authors as either functional attributes (intrinsic characteristics of servant-leaders) or accompanying attributes (complement attributes that enhance the functional attributes).[4] The operational attributes were identified as vision, honesty, integrity, trust, modeling, service, pioneering, appreciation, and empowerment with the accompanying attributes of communication, credibility, competence, stewardship, visibility, influence, persuasion, listening, encouragement, teaching, and delegation. Only three of the attributes identified by Greenleaf were identified, and all three were accompanying attributes rather than functional. Responsibility, adaptability, affection, discipleship, navigation, and reproduction attributes which are considered critical in biblical-based servant leadership in my LSL model are not covered by Russell and Greenleaf. As shown in the description of the attributes in Table 1.2, most of the attributes reported by Russell and Stone (2002)[5] or Greenleaf [1] can be seen either in the twenty attributes or their associated characteristics. Integrity and honesty for example are leadership characteristics of trust and other attributes rather than an independent attributes. I take the position that servant leadership attributes are functional attributes in acts of duty to others and emanate from the inner value system of the leader.

CHAPTER 1
UNDERSTANDING LEADERSHIP ATTRIBUTES

Table 1.2: Description of the functional leader-servant outward leadership attributes and associated principles and characteristics

Leader–Servant Leadership Attributes	Principles of Leadership Attributes	Leadership Characteristics
Affection: *This is the combined love-based works toward providing the essential help or services for the spiritual growth or survival of another person. .* (Chapter 2)	*Affection flows from a person to produce positive emotions for the well-being of another person*	Kindness Compassion Practical Love Affective signs Appreciation
Discipleship: *This is the combined acts of personally developing, intentionally equipping, and attentively empowering growth in others to reproduce a heart of service.* (Chapter 3)	*Discipleship transforms and empowers followers for service leadership that grows communities.*	Inspiring Shepherding Equipping Developing Empowering
Emulation: *This is the combined acts of initiating an authentic servant attitude as a model of service worthy of following* (Chapter 4)	*A great leader-servant outwardly and positively inspires a pattern of good works for others to follow.*	Inspiration Motivation Initiation Model Following
Generosity: *This is the combined acts of freely sharing with and giving to others as an act of kindness, without expectation of reward or return to him.* (Chapter 5)	*Generosity is an outward measure of the level of sacrifice, what is shared, or the impact a giving makes, not just the size of the giving.*	Sharing Giving Kindness Affection Love
Healing-Care: *This is the combined acts of providing comfort and empathy to make others whole emotionally and spiritually along with tending to the follower's physical and mental well-being.* (Chapter 6)	*Comforting others in any trouble with the comfort with which we are comforted by God, brings healing - wholeness.*	Self- Healing Empathy Reconciliation Comfort Relational
Influence: *This is the combined acts of positively affecting desired change in conduct,*	*The true measure of leadership success in affecting*	Model Positive attitude Authority

ALS DISCIPLESHIP LEADERSHIP
ATTRIBUTES, PRINCIPLES, & PRACTICES

performance, and relational connections toward others-centered course of action or service. (Chapter 7)	*desired change in conduct, performance, and relational connections in others is influence*	Connection Wisdom Intelligence,
Persuasion: *This is the combined acts of communicating perspective to connect, challenge, and convince with a compelling purpose to convert others to a new position.* (Chapter 8)	*The means of transforming others to a new perspective is through empathetic persuasion*	Connecting Challenging Communicating Convincing Converting Encouraging
Reproduction: *This is the combined acts of developing your leadership qualities in others and releasing them as successors to continue a greater mission.* (Chapter 9)	*Great leaders produce successors for legacy and greater courses as an expected product of an effective leadership reproduction.*	Selecting Mentoring Equipping Empowering Releasing
Servanthood: *This is the combined acts of humility, willingness, and intentionality in service to others through selfless sacrifice and submission as a servant.* (Chapter 10)	*A leader-servant is most qualified to lead when most ready to serve as a servant for the growth of others. The role of a leader is to serve as a servant*	Servant's heart Humility Sacrifice Service Willingness Submissiveness
Trust: *This is the combined acts of positive display of character, competence, credibility, and shared relational connections that produce assured trust-confidence of the trustee in the trusted.* (Chapter 11)	*True leadership trust produces assured trustee's confidence and readiness to follow based on the credibility, competence, and shared relational connections of the trusted.*	Character Competence Integrity Credibility Confidence

PRINCIPLE OF LEADERSHIP ATTRIBUTE

In the context of servant leadership, a leadership attribute is a level above the leadership characteristic or trait of a leader. The principle of leadership attribute states that every leadership attribute has a set of distinguishing characteristics that make up the inward or outward display of the attribute. The principle reflects the essential designed purpose or outcome of the attribute or the inevitable consequence of the effective practice of the attribute. Thus, the principle of leadership attribute is a concise statement about the fundamental truth, value, or belief about the attribute in a leadership situation; it is a statement that establishes an idea about the outcome of the attribute for guiding the practical application of the attribute and its characteristics. I will postulate and frame each principle as an additive function of the characteristics of the attribute. A statement of each principle is quoted at the beginning or below the title of each chapter. It is yet to be experimentally proven if the attribute is a linear or some other non-linear function of these characteristics as variables. It is expected, however, that each character will contribute to the effectiveness of the attribute in varying degrees.

AUTHENTIC LEADERSHIP ATTRIBUTES

At a personal level, attributes are the value-based inside-out moral leadership assets that can be related to the authenticity of a leader-servant. The complexity of defining authenticity has been noted in the literature. The subject of authentic leadership is well covered in the works of Terry (1993),[5] George (2003),[6] and Shair and Eilam (2005).[7] All appear to agree that authenticity requires self-awareness and objective self-identity in personal and social interactions with others. In his book, *Advocacy Leadership*, Professor Gary L. Anderson offers individual, organizational, and societal perspectives on authenticity: "Authenticity, at a peculiar level, is living a life, whether in the private or professional term. This is congruent with one's espoused values; at the structural level, authenticity has to do with viewing human beings as ends in themselves, rather than means to other ends; at the public level, it is a state of affairs that is congruous with the shared political and cultural values of society."[8]

The basic tenets of these perspectives are very fitting to authenticity as a qualifying element of leader-servant leadership attributes. The attribute reflects how the followers see the leader based on the leader's distinctive features displayed through his or her actions personally, organizationally, and societally. The leader is seen as a leader-servant or serving leader because the followers see him lead as a servant from an inside-out value of others. This is what makes the leader authentic. Authenticity means that what a leader displays outside, in personal or leadership life of service to others, and society is based on the values the leader espouses inside.

Authenticity in servant leadership can be one or two types or both: *Outbound Authenticity and Outward Authenticity*. The Outbound (outward-bound) Authenticity is the genuineness of personal honesty from your inner strength and abilities; what you say and how you act emanate from who you are or how you feel inside. It reflects the essential truth and honesty about your outward-bound inner strength.

Outward authenticity, on the other hand, describes the truthfulness of your credibility and honesty displayed outward in relation to others; your *outer* visible behavior or how you act outwardly towards others reflects exactly your true intentions.

While *outward* authenticity is the visible *outer* indicator of the truth of who you are inside, *outbound* authenticity is outward-bound attribute from the inside of who you are. Credibility in this context is the influence a leader has to attract believability, trustworthiness, and authenticity; it is the believability, trustworthiness, and authenticity of who you are inside and outside.

A key element of personal authenticity is that it is seen or measured in the context of societal, cultural, and organizational interactions. In that context, achieving individual authenticity becomes a challenge since it is influenced by social factors and dispositions of individuals who usually depend on liberal and organizational realities. However, for leader-servant leadership, the leader can face those changing times by remaining focused on his key Biblical-based principles or *Leadership Inner Value System*. Thus, I am interested in authenticity as an essential element of effective Leader-servant leadership attributes or Leader-servant leadership attributes as drivers of leadership authenticity. With that in mind, the first critical element of authenticity in practicing or developing efficient leader-servant leadership attributes is inside-out self-examination relative to the people served rather than the organization. You may ask yourself: What will be my response when the people I lead act or react in a certain way, will it be negative or positive? What are my strengths and vulnerabilities at those times?

Professor Yacobi in his post, "Elements of Human Authenticity," noted that since "the self -arise attribute emerges from interactions between self, others, and the environment in a complex society and world, there may co-exist multiple complicated identities depending on place and context." [9] He went on to identify the following <u>essential elements of personal authenticity</u>: self-awareness, unbiased self-examination, accurate self-knowledge, reflective judgment, personal responsibility, and integrity, genuineness, and humility, empathy for others, understanding of others, optimal utilization of feedback from others. All of these are covered under the leadership attributes or characteristics shown in Table 1.2.

Bill George, in his book, *Authentic Leadership*, takes the position that to be an authentic leader; a person must have the following essential characteristics: [10]

- Behavior based on value: He must understand his own values and exhibit behavior to others based on those values;
- He must not compromise his values in difficult situations but could use the situation to strengthen personal values in those situations.
- Passion from a clear purpose: Be self-aware of who he is, where he is going, and the right thing to do.
- Compassion from the heart: He must lead from a compassionate heart that allows them to be sensitive to the plight and needs of others,
- Connectedness from a relationship; he must be relationally connected with people he leads,
- Consistency from the self-disciple: He must demonstrate self-discipline to remain calm, collected, and consistent in a stressful situation.

Modeled after the elements above, Table 1.3 lists six essential characteristics of authenticity for servant leadership. These fundamental characteristics cover the five identified above and can also be aligned with the leadership characteristics in Table 1.2. Each attribute in Table 1.2 is expected to pass the personal authenticity test in Tables 1.3, 1.4. In a survey of 132 Christian leaders, seventy-four percent (74%) of them agreed that they always or frequently exhibit servant leadership attributes. [11] Thus, a pass of the outward authenticity test means that a pure leader must demonstrate 70% or more of these essential elements of this legitimacy. (That is, 70% YES in the assessment questions in Tables 1.3, 1.4).

It needs to be noted, however, that a secular leader could be authentic and still lack some of the essential servant leadership attributes or characteristics such as selflessness, servanthood, and love-motivated servant attitudes of a leader-servant. Effective leader-servants are authentic leaders and personal authenticity is an essential element of leader-servant leadership. The key test for leader-servant authenticity is the quality of his inside-out value and personal character. What is most important is a change from the inside-out.

	Table 1.3: The test of essential elements of personal inner strength authenticity in servant leadership		
	Elements of Inner Strength Authenticity	**Inner Strength (Outbound) Authenticity Assessment Questions**	**YES / NO**
1	Personal inside-out value-based behavior	Are your personal inside-out values aligned with acts of service and behavior outside?	1
		Are you honest to yourself in relation to your inner strengths and abilities?	2
2	Inside-out Self-Awareness	Do you have unbiased self-examination, and accurate self-knowledge of who you are inside-out?	3
		Do you know your inner strength and weaknesses in relation to the good you want to show as an outward attribute?	4
3	Inside-out Empathy-Compassion	Do you know and feel from your inside what you want for your followers?	5
		Are you motivated to empathize, based on your inside feelings?	6
4	Inside-out Connection with followers	Do you feel deep, personal, and spiritual connection with your followers?	7
		Does what you say and how you act reflect how you feel when you relate to others?	8
5	Inside-out Emotional Self-regulation	Do you have difficulty controlling your emotion in order to remain calm in a stressful situation?	9
		Are you always able to comfort yourself?	10
6	Inside-out Authenticity Feedback	Do your followers see your inside-out value from your outside behavior?	11
		Will your followers feel that what you say you are is congruent with how you act?	12
	#YESs_____ ; # NOs_____ : Outbound Authenticity: YES/ 12————%		

CHAPTER 1
UNDERSTANDING LEADERSHIP ATTRIBUTES

Table 1.4: The test of essential elements of personal outward authenticity in servant leadership

	Elements of Personal Outward Authenticity	Personal Outward Authenticity Assessment Questions	YES or NO
1	Personal value-based outward behavior	Are your personal values and beliefs aligned with your acts of service and behavior toward others?	1
		Do you live out your life according to your beliefs?	2
2	Personal Self-Awareness	Do you have clarity of your personal vision and purpose?	3
		Does what you know about yourself accurately describe what others say?	4
3	Personal Outward Empathy-Compassion	Do you apply how you feel to what your followers need?	5
		Do you lead from a compassionate heart and are you sensitive to the plight and needs of others?	6
4	Personal Connection with followers	Do you feel deep, personal connection with your followers?	7
		Does your outward action toward others reflect exactly your true intentions?	8
5	Outward Emotional Self-regulation	Do you have difficulty controlling your emotions to remain calm in a stressful situation?	9
		Does your evaluation of your value of others agree with how valued they feel?	10
6	Personal Authenticity Feedback	Do your followers see your outward acts as true and honest?	11
		Can your followers see other-centeredness in 70% or more of your attributes?	12

#YESs_____; # NOs_____; Outward Authenticity: YES/12————%

Table 1.5. Leader As Servant-Leadership Audit

A servant-leader in his leadership position purposefully choses to serve and inspire acts of service in others by his example. Select and circle best answer to questions
1=Never; 2=Almost never; 3=Sometimes; 4=Frequently; 5 =Always

	Servant Leadership assessment questions	Circle no
1	I am willing and other-centered, and readily chose to serve others as a servant for their personal growth	1 2 3 4 5
2	I model others-centered attitude in my service and relationships and inspire same for others to follow	1 2 3 4 5
3	I have a sense of obligation, willingness, and accountability for the service towards others	1 2 3 4 5
4	I have the foresightedness to specify in the present view what others' growth should be in a given future	1 2 3 4 5
5	I work toward providing the essential help or services for the spiritual growth or survival of the others;	1 2 3 4 5
6	I provide the needed purposeful course of action for how to chart the course to for my followers.	1 2 3 4 5
7	I display external credibility and a strong sense of character based on values, beliefs, and competence;	1 2 3 4 5
8	In communication, I attentively perceive and hear what is communicated, reflectively listen to understand and to be understood	1 2 3 4 5
9	I walk through with others in their state (suffering, emotions, etc.) in a way that provides the needed care and well-being	1 2 3 4 5
10	I have a measure of self-secured flexibility to adapt appropriate attitude to serve all people in different situations	1 2 3 4 5
11	I personally develop, intentionally equip, and attentively nurture spiritually growth in others	1 2 3 4 5
12	My act of bravery instills in others the courage and confidence to follow or persevere in a course of action	1 2 4 5
13	I develop my leadership qualities in others as successors to continue in a purposeful mission	1 2 3 4 5
14	I manage, maintain,, and account for all resources entrusted to me and being responsible for the difference my acts make	1 2 3 4 5
15	As a care-giver, I act to comfort and make others whole emotionally	1 2 3 4 5
16	When I see a need, I originate a vision and action, and stay committed to meet that need and desired change	1 2 3 4 5

17	I display a holistic view of an issue to inform, transform or convert others to my view through empathetic persuasion	1	2	3	4	5
18	I freely share what I have sacrificially as an act of kindness to others, without expectation of reward in return	1	2	3	4	5
19	My act of influence is to affect the actions, behavior, opinions, etc., of others based on trust, credibility and relationship	1	2	3	4	5
20	In the face challenges and danger, I act with bravery to overcome fear and take a stand with strength and conviction	1	2	3	4	5
Score Range	Add up the numbers in each column (Total Score____) Check and Understand the key areas to work on					
81-100	Strong Leader-Servant; keep it up, go and train others.					
66-80	Above average Leader-Servant; work 25% of key areas					
50-65	Average but developing; need to work on 50% of key areas					
34-49	Below average leader; work on 75% of key areas					
<34	Not a Leader-Servant; need training in all areas					

Summary 1
Understanding Leadership Process

Before starting this exercise, please read and follow the instruction in the preface of this workbook. Answers to these questions are contained in this chapter. Completion of these exercises after reading the chapter should take 60-90 minutes.

Discovering the Leadership Attributes

1. What is your alternative definition of leadership? In learning to lead, how would you differentiate the following elements:
    a. Leadership,
    b. Leader as servant leadership.
    c. Leadership characteristics.
    d. Leadership attributes
2. How should you lead in the context of this chapter?

Understanding the Leadership Principles

1. Define or state the principle of Servanthood Leadership attribute. How true is that in your leadership experience?
2. What are the key differences between the Leader as Servant and the Servant as Leader Leadership philosophies?
3. How can you display the essential qualities of authentic leader in a leadership process in challenging times.?
4. What are the characteristics of a leader-servant?
5. What was the original source of the Servant as Leader (SL)? What was the original source of Leader as Servant (LS)?
6. How do you compare the two model characters of Leo in SL and Jesus in LS
7. What is the key framework of a Leader as a Servant Leadership?

Practicing Authentic Leadership

1. Authenticity in servant leadership can be one or two types or both *Outbound Authenticity and Outward Authenticity*: Describe a time when you displayed:
    a. The Outbound (outward-bound)— *outbound* authenticity is outward-bound attribute from the inside of who you are.
    b. *The Outward Authenticity*—*outward* authenticity is the visible *outer* indicator of the truth of who you are inside,
2. Describe the key elements of personal authenticity seen or measured in the context of societal, cultural, and organizational interactions.
3. Take the outbound (Table 1.3) and Outward (Table 1.4) leadership authenticity tests. How (%) authentic are you (#YES/12) in each measure in your leadership process?
4. In the elements you rated as NO, review the relevant passage, learn what is missing in you and write a personal commitment statement on how to work to improve in those areas
5. How much of a leader-servant are you? Take the personal leader-servant audit in Table 1.5 to self-assess your effectiveness.
6. Based on the questions in Table 1.5, can you identify each of the twenty attributes? What ones did you score 3 ("sometimes") or less than 3? Review and learn and commit to work to improve.

CHAPTER 2
LEADERSHIP DISCIPLESHIP
LEADERSHIP ATTRIBUTE

Discipleship transforms and empowers followers for service leadership that grows communities.

Discipleship as an act of developing a follower toward a specific goal is an important function of leadership to equip others to lead. The "others" being disciples by a leader-servant are usually referred to as disciples or followers being trained by a master. A disciple is a follower who willingly chooses to follow the master and submits to his discipleship and authority. In that regard, Jesus wanted all his followers to be his disciples and ambassadors because a disciple is always a follower. Organizationally, a follower could be a junior employee, any employee in a brand-new department, a new younger faculty, or just any person that needs to be guided through a journey of professional growth and good success. This chapter will focus on the general growth of followers through the acts of discipleship and presents the critical characteristics of discipleship as a leadership outward attribute. Functional definitions of leadership discipleship attributes and its principle will be presented based on those characteristics. Each characteristic will be discussed in detail with emphasis on strategies of how they can be further developed or practiced as a part of the servant leadership process.

CHARACTERISTICS OF DISCIPLESHIP ATTRIBUTE

Jesus taught His disciples the characters expected of those desiring to be His true disciples:

> *"Whoever wants to be my disciple must deny themselves and take up their cross and follow me. [25] For whoever wants to save their life will lose it, but whoever loses their life for me will find it. What good will it be for someone to gain the whole world, yet forfeit their soul? Or what can anyone give in exchange for their soul?..." (Mathew 16:24-27, NIV).*

Jesus said that if you desire to be His disciple, your attitude and character must outwardly display the following actions:

Self-deny yourself: You must, by your own free will, renounce yourself of riches, honor, and pleasure, must and voluntarily surrender everything that might hinder your discipleship. You must deny wrongful self, ungodliness, worldly lusts, and all former sinful associations; you must deny all works of self-righteousness, desires for profits of this world that could be competition with Christ; you must do all for the sake of your Lord, and Master, Jesus. Organizationally, self-denial means putting others' needs ahead of yours and rejecting any personal desires that will hinder you from the performance of your assigned responsibilities.

Take up your cross daily: You must be determined to bear your suffering of the walk, including service to others; you must prepare for persecution, suffering, and all challenges. You must bear the Lord's suffering, shame, and death, and must be ready to endure it, and rejoice in it; and you must have a sense of worthiness for and belonging to the cross of Jesus. To take up your cross also means being able to endure hardships, disappointments, and a setback for whatever work you are in.

Follow the Master: You should always with patience, and self-denial morally discharges the obligated duties of a disciple of Jesus. The same principle can be applied in the workplace for that young staff members or junior faculty. You must be humble enough to follow the good example and discipleship of people that have gone before you as if they are your masters. To be an effective follower, you must passionately, actively, and zealously follow the master's footsteps, bearing in mind that his footsteps may lead to challenges but will always lead to a greater reward. I have had my students complain, and cry at the level of expectations and culture of excellence I put forward for their walkthrough during their undergraduate education. All have come back to appreciate the opportunity to follow and measure up to those challenges when they see how better prepared they were in meeting them. An effective master or mentor understands the pathway and visualizes the journey much further than the follower can possibly see. Spiritual discipleship by the leader-servant of his followers involves developing these three qualities in the five interconnected stages of action of a leader-servant:

The leader *shepherds* the disciples by providing security, guidance, and immediate sustenance to remain in spiritual oneness with God. The "shepherd-ship" or shepherding process focuses on protecting and guiding the selected disciples from going astray or getting lost. Shepherd-ship is not only caring for the followers' needs but also involves finding that one lost sheep and helping to bring it back to the fold. Some characteristics of shepherding skills include *love, nurturing, relational maintenance, and spiritual care.*

The leader *develops* the disciples by spiritually building up followers to become Christ-like or better versions of themselves; the leader-servant's acts of discipleship will lead the disciples, especially those that are brand new believers, and spiritually train their characters and grow their talents or develop new ones to build a thriving Christian community. Jesus mainly used his teaching, miracle healing, life examples, and interactions with people to influence change toward Christ-likeness. The leader willingly and eagerly commits to serving the flock of God or the community of believers by caring for and guiding them to grow collectively.

The leader *equips* the disciples. After developing and training their character for service, the leader must equip followers for the ministry. For example, Jesus equipped his disciples by inspiring each to take up his own cross to follow Him, providing them with Servant leadership examples and a pattern to follow. He also fostered opportunities such as feeding the four thousand to show how real service for God includes the faith that God provides for all needs, even in times of challenge and uncertainty (Mark 8:1-21).

The leader *empowers* the disciples. Unless the disciples are empowered to reproduce, the shepherding, developing, and equipping will have no impact. To empower is to commission followers to go and serve, such as the promise of the power of the Holy Spirit, for ministry. It also means allocating power or responsibility to followers to demonstrate their training and growth, engaging followers in their own growth, influencing the transformation of self to serve, and empowering mastery of skills by increased self-efficacy.

The leader's discipleship *reproduces* other leaders. This is usually the ultimate goal of discipleship—to lead a follower through a process of developing himself or herself. This also involves a good measure of *mentoring*.

PRINCIPLE OF DISCIPLINE ATTRIBUTE

In summary, the leader-servant shepherd develops, equips, empowers, reproduces, and mentors. The effectiveness of spiritual discipleship is that it impacts the disciples and their outside communities and results in the desired change toward reproducing Christ-likeness in others. Based on the above characteristics my working definition is as follows:

> *Servant leadership discipleship attribute is the combined acts of personally developing, intentionally equipping, and attentively empowering growth in others to reproduce a heart of service.*

The catalyst that initiates any affective action is the love of God and obedience to His command to love, even our enemies. Based on these characteristics, I come to the following definition:

> *Servant leadership affection attribute is the combined love-based work toward providing the essential help or services for the spiritual growth or survival of another person.*

Leadership discipleship outward attribute is displayed in stages involving some elements of Servant leadership. In the case of Jesus, the spiritual discipleship of His followers, the twelve disciples, in particular, resulted in opening the eyes and ears of many Influencers and influencing the desired spiritual growth and transformation of hearts. It also allowed the newly changed hearts to apply the brand new knowledge in their lives and others. Based on the above characteristics and the desired outcome of the effective servant-leadership discipleship attribute, a principle emerges and can be stated as follows:

Discipleship transforms and empowers followers for service leadership that grows communities.

This principle means that the act of discipleship transforms and equips followers to grow spiritually to reproduce Christlikeness through a four-stage addictive process shown in Figure 3 and expressed as:

PERSONAL + INTENTIONAL + ATTENTIVE + REPRODUCTIVE = DISCIPLESHIP

SUMMARY 2
LEADERSHIP DISCIPLESHIP
LEADERSHIP ATTRIBUTE

Before starting this exercise, please read and follow the instruction in the preface of this workbook. Answers to these questions are contained in this chapter. Completion of these exercises after reading the chapter should take 60-90 minutes.

Discovering Discipleship Leadership Attributes

1. Define discipleship.
2. What is the difference between a disciple and a follower?
3. How is discipleship a leadership outward attribute?
4. What are the five stages in which Leadership discipleship outward attribute is displayed?
5. What did Jesus teach His disciples to be the characters expected of those desiring to be His true disciples: *(Mathew 16:24-27, NIV)*?
6. What are the distinguishing characteristics of Discipleship Attribute?

7. What is spiritual discipleship What three qualities in the five interconnected stages of action of a leader-servant are involved in spiritual discipleship?
8. What is the goal result in discipleship as exemplified by Jesus?

Principle of Discipleship Attribute

1. Define *Servant leadership discipleship attribute*
2. State the principle of discipleship attribute
3. State the additive law of discipleship attribute
4. What does this principle mean in the context of leader-servant leadership?

Practicing Discipleship Leadership Attribute

1. What would you consider the key characteristics of discipleship leadership attributes?
2. How many acts of discipleship as an attribute do you display? Discipleship leadership attribute audit in Table 2.
3. Based on the questions in Table 2 can you identify each of the acts of generosity leadership attribute? What ones did you score 3 ("sometimes") or less than 3? Review and learn and commit to work to improve

CHAPTER 2
LEADERSHIP DISCIPLESHIP LEADERSHIP ATTRIBUTE

Table 2. Leadership Discipleship Attribute Audit

Servant leadership discipleship attribute is the combined acts of personally developing, intentionally equipping, and attentively empowering growth in others to reproduce a heart of service. Assess the quality of your acts of discipleship attribute by inserting an X below the number that best describes your response to each statement.

Item	Acts of Affection Attribute Check 1= Always; 2= Frequently; 3= Sometimes; 4= Almost Never; 5= Never	1	2	3	4	5
1	I develop followers by one-on-one engagement					
2	I personally mentor, equip, and empower growth and heart of service in others					
3	I show followers a pattern to follow to model their lives					
4	I develop followers to become great leaders					
5	I make deliberate selfless act to motivate others					
6	My intentional acts of discipleship are purposefully directed to equip followers for growth					
7	I guard the followers against false teachings from within or outside					
8	I give close attention to nurture the spiritual growth in others.					
9	I am usually able to discern and determine the needs of the followers					
10	I create opportunities to encourage followers to practice what they know or have learned.					
	Add up your rating in each column					
Total Score	Guide and Explanation of Score: understand the areas you need to further develop			Total		
10-17	Great discipleship leader; keep it up!
18-25	Above Average affection; need to work 25% of the areas
26-33	Average affection; need to need to work on 50% of the areas
34-41	Below average- affection, need to work on 75% of the key areas
42-50	Not affectionate; Seek counseling, work in all the areas

CHAPTER 3
DEVELOPING THE ACTS OF PERSONAL DISCIPLESHIP

The process of Spiritual Discipleship starts with individual discipleship. Personal discipleship involves the one-on-one engagement of a leader to develop Christ-likeness in another person, usually a believer. It involves making an individual commitment to the spiritual growth of a follower. The following are four levels of intimate actions you can take to disciple others

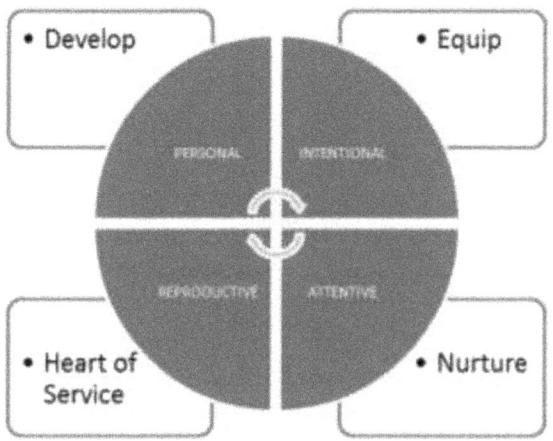

Figure 3: Four cyclic process models of spiritual discipleship disciple-attribute

Willingly love and share yourself as a mother

Personal engagement in discipleship is like a mother's willingness to care for the development of an infant child. Paul told the Thessalonians, "Instead, we were like young children among you. Just as a nursing mother cares for her children, so we cared for you. Because we loved you so much, we were delighted to share with you not only the gospel of God but our lives as well" (1 Thessalonians 2:7-8, NIV). Note that the reason for making a personal commitment to care for others is like the love for a child or a disciple. That love delightfully motivates the leader-servant, like a mother shares her milk, to apportion the Gospel and his life with the believer. For example, in my mentoring students, to disciple younger Christians in the fellowship, or couples in marriage situations, I have learned that nothing influences change more than honestly and openly sharing my personal life with them. Sometimes students are discouraged and almost hopeless as they walk into my office, but they leave motivated and inspired. For example, one of my graduate students visited me after he had qualified and left the school, and was doing some great things. He came to show me appreciation. He told me a story, tearing up as he spoke, how he came to my office one day to announce that he was quitting his graduate studies; indeed, he could not handle the research anymore. He told me that when I opened up to him and shared my personal experiences—my fears, failures, and how my faith changed my mountain of difficulties—he said to himself, "This man does not know what I am going through." Even so, by the time I finished speaking with him, he was already repositioning his mind for success. He said he stood up and left, but was inspired by the thought that if Professor Wosu made it with so many obstacles, he could also achieve it too. Honestly sharing your experiences, especially the very tearful ones with your followers and those to whom you are accountable, is extremely good to impact in encouraging them in their own situations. This example may not be the same as leading a follower for Christ in discipleship, but the process or impact of sharing works the same in each case.

Instruct and encourage one-on-one like a father

In the same way, a father gives particular encouragement and direction to a son. The leader-servant personally implores each believer to take on Christ-likeness or purposefully follow those steps that will propel him or her to a desired positive destination. The instruction to encourage must be purposeful and direct. Paul wrote; "Just as you know how we were exhorting and encouraging and imploring each one of you as a father would his own children so that you would walk in a manner worthy of the God who calls you into His own kingdom and glory"(1 Thessalonian 2:11-12, NIV). One thing is clear here: Paul was very personal and was there with them in the flesh, looking into their

Chapter 3
Developing the Acts of Personal Discipleship

eyes and instructing them. Although we recognize the impact of technology such as Skype, web-based meetings, email, and so on, nothing can substitute for face-to-face sharing and the associated instant assessment and feedback that indicate how the process is going. Personal discipleship requires this type of commitment to be effective. Nothing can substitute for this kind of hand-holding, an individual touch of a respected leader-servant pouring himself into another person's life. A sense that the leader personally cares in a father-son type relationship is a powerful motivation for the follower to trust and submit to his discipleship.

Commit daily to follower's growth

Just like in the case of Paul, you must personally commit daily to the spiritual and professional growth and welfare of your followers. Anyone who has mentored someone will agree that the cost and commitment in discipleship are different and higher because of the everyday requirements, the stress, and the one-on-one walk. Paul was happy to expend himself to see growth in followers as he told them; "I will most gladly spend and be spent for your souls. If I love you more, am I to be loved less? (2 Corinthians 12:15, ESV). You must personally, not as part of a group, be involved in the welfare of your disciples—their interests, their sufferings, and their successes. You must find time to visit and bear with them in their states of suffering helping them bear their sorrows or celebrate with them to show that you care for their progress.

Show followers a pattern to follow to model their lives

As the saying goes, "experience is the best teacher." The experience becomes even a better teacher when a leader truthfully patterns favorable examples in real-time. The followers should actually see or walk with the leader who displays those positive attributes such as the treatment of others, handling responsibilities, balancing life schedule for high productivity, and the quality of work, etc. Speaking to the Philippians believers, Paul said, "Dear brothers and sisters, pattern your lives after mine, and learn from those who follow our example" (Philippians 3:17, NLT). Paul wanted them to continue to model what he had taught them from what he also learned from Christ.

Urge the follower to be imitators: "For I became your father in Christ Jesus through the gospel. I urge you, then, be imitators of me" (1 Corinthians 4:15-16). Paul urged his followers to mimic him even as he emulated Christ. Leaders must be intentional in urging and inspiring followers to follow their pattern for good success and must make the followers see in them those examples that are worthy of imitating. Showing followers a pattern to follow to model their lives might involve leaders opening themselves up for followers to be free to ask questions and being ready to use every opportunity the follower sees as a teaching moment for growth.

SUMMARY 3
DEVELOPING THE ACTS OF PERSONAL DISCIPLINE INSTRUCTION

Before starting this exercise, please read and follow the instruction in the preface of this workbook. Answers to these questions are contained in this chapter. Completion of these exercises after reading the chapter should take 60-90 minutes.

Discovering the Acts of Personal Discipleship

1. What are involved in Personal discipleship?
2. What are the four levels of intimate actions you can take to disciple others
3. Personal engagement in discipleship is like a mother's willingness to care for the development of an infant child. How did Apostle Paul illustrate personal discipleship in (1 Thessalonians 2:7-12, NIV).
4. In what ways was Apostle Paul personal in these passages?
5. What is the most effective way you have influenced change in people?

Practicing Acts of Personal Discipleship Attribute

Persional Discipleship involves the personal one-to-one engagement of a leader to develop Christlikeness in another person usually a believer.

CHAPTER 3
DEVELOPING THE ACTS OF PERSONAL DISCIPLESHIP

1. Develop a four-stage personal plan you can use as a leader for the discipleship of others.
2. List a few strategies to be considered starting from individual disciples to the community of disciples or leaders:
3. How does a leader commission the disciples to go and multiply?
4. One strategy in practicing acts of discipleship is to commit daily to follower's growth. What did Apostle Paul suggest we follow in this concept (2 Corinthians 12:15, ESV).
5. Personal Discipleship also involved showing followers a pattern to follow to model their lives. Speaking to the Philippians believers, Paul said, "Dear brothers and sisters, pattern your lives after mine, and learn from those who follow our example" (Philippians 3:17, NLT) or in (1 Corinthians 4:15-16). What was Paul urging his followers to do?

CHAPTER 4
DEVELOPING THE ACTS OF INTENTIONAL DISCIPLESHIP

Earlier, I defined intentionality as a leader's deliberate selflessness motivated by the love to serve others. For example, Jesus, in his intentional commitment to disciple his followers, was calculated in washing the disciples' feet. Some of the drivers for intentionality in a leader-servant are value, focus, decisiveness, and individual commitment. As it relates to discipleship, personal commitment is a great start but leads nowhere unless there is purposeful action deliberately directed to the believer's growth. Thus, intentional spiritual discipleship means that it is not coincidental or accidental but purposefully directed to equipping the disciple with a pre-determined outcome.

STRATEGIES FOR INTENTIONAL DISCIPLESHIP

Intentionally equip the disciple with sound teaching and training. Intentional discipleship focuses on purposely equipping the disciple with sound teaching and training to reproduce desired knowledge for ministry and personal growth. Speaking to believers in Ephesus, Paul taught what leaders must do in discipleship. "to equip his people for works of service, so that the body of Christ may be built up until we all reach unity in the faith and the knowledge of the Son of God and become mature..."(Ephesians 4:11-16). Applying the same principle to any organization, intentional equipping of a follower could mean taking a conscious effort to focus on equipping the follower with needed teaching, training, information, and resources to reproduce the desired expectations in any setting. It means being accountable for what the follower's functional needs are for expected growth.

To be intentional, the service for which the leader must equip the followers and the expected results must be specified clearly and planned purposefully. Leaders are to equip followers for service that will yield desired results, including Building faith and knowledge of

Christ; growing spiritually and professionally, and building a thriving others-centered community.

Although personal commitment is one-on-one, intentional commitment can involve others as an act of individual commitment and may require the leader to solicit the involvement of other trusted teachers or leaders to help followers see their growth and the fruit ahead of them and beyond them.

Intentionally guard the followers against false teachings from within or outside. A leader-servant as an excellent shepherd protects the sheep from all internal or external influence or danger. "I am the good shepherd; I know my sheep and my sheep know me, and I lay down my life for the sheep" (John 10:14-18, NIV). A good shepherd puts the sheep before himself and has no limits to the sacrifices he makes for the sheep's welfare. He values and protects the sheep and knows the sheep, and the sheep know him (John 10:11-13). In the same passage, Jesus talked about wolves scattering the sheep. How do we apply this principle? Paul gave specific instructions to leaders on how to guard against these wolves in the form of false teachers and doctrines. He said; "Pay careful attention to yourselves and to all the flock, in which the Holy Spirit has made you overseers, to care for the church of God, which he obtained with his own blood ... be alert, remembering that for three years I did not cease night or day to admonish every one with tears"(Acts 20:28-31, ESV). The lessons to be learned from these passages include: leaders must intentionally pay prudent attention to what they do and to the member of the flock, that is, pay attention to whom and what they listen to. The leader is accountable for what happens to the flock in terms of the knowledge they are gaining; they must be guarded to beware of fierce wolves that will come among them to destroy the flock; the follower, especially the younger/junior ones. The Leader must be aware of deceitful or misleading teachers among them or those with those they do not share the same goal, and they must be vigilant about false teaching from within the organization and also outside.

Intentionally focus on followers bearing Christ-like fruit. Intentionally equipping followers with sound teaching and knowledge is not enough in discipleship. There must be an intentional focus on the direction of bearing Christ-like fruit and helping them see their growth and fruit both ahead of them and beyond. For example, to the believers in Colossian Paul wrote: "The gospel is bearing fruit and growing throughout the whole world… his will…so that you may live a life worthy of the Lord and please him in every way: bearing fruit in every good work, growing in the knowledge of God" (Colossian 1:6 - 10, NIV). Several intentional actions in discipleship can be drawn from this passage: intentionally focusing on bearing fruit, continuously praying for the followers, consecutively asking God to fill them with the knowledge of His will, helping those who bear fruit in every good work, and growing in the knowledge of God. This is true in any organization in which leaders want growth in the followers. For good success as a measure of beneficial fruit, the leader must strategically position the followers to see the journey for their growth ahead and align the progress toward the goals with the resources, assistance, and mentoring they will need.

SUMMARY 4
DEVELOPING THE ACTS OF INTERNATIONAL DISCIPLESHIP

Before starting this exercise, please read and follow the instruction in the preface of this workbook. Answers to these questions are contained in this chapter. Completion of these exercises after reading the chapter should take 60-90 minutes.

Discovering the Acts of Intentional Discipleship

1. Define intentionality.
2. What was intentional Jesus actions in his disciple of his followers?
3. What does Intentional spiritual discipleship mean in the context of equipping the disciple?

Practicing Intentional Discipleship

1. **Intentional Discipleship** is a deliberate selfless act of a leader motivated by love to serve others.
    a. Why and how can intentional discipleship be directed to the equipping of the disciple with a pre-determined outcome?

b. What is the purpose of Intentionally equipping the disciple with sound biblical teaching
2. Intentionally equipping the disciple with sound teaching and training is one strategy presented for Intentional discipleship.
    a. How did Apostle Pau illustrate this in his teachings? (Ephesians 4:11-16).
    b. How can you apply this principle to any organization you know?
3. What is the role of a leader to intentionally guard the followers against false teachings from within or outside? (see John 10:11-13). s Acts 20:28-31, ESV).
4. What lessons are to be learned from these passages with respect to intentionality
5. Practicing Intentional discipleship also involves focus on the direction for bearing Christ-like fruit and helping them see their growth and fruit both ahead of them and beyond.
    a. How does the scripture exemplify this in (Colossian 1:6 -10, NIV)?
    b. How have you practiced this in your personal life?

CHAPTER 5
DEVELOPING THE ACTS OF ATTENTIVE DISCIPLESHIP

Attentive discipleship is the act of giving close attention to sustaining unworldly growth in others as a mother nurtures a newborn. Spiritual discipleship relates to developing new believers, and attentive commitment calls for giving them the type of near observation newborn needs. Although personal care is critical at the beginning, a larger community may be involved as the process advances. This is why it is important not to ignore individual needs such as those of younger/junior believers or followers when they are in a greater group.

Discern the Needs of your Followers

Discerning needs in the context of servant leadership is the process of determining God's purpose or desire in the follower's life or helping the individual discern his or her life's purpose or calling. This is not the same as "the discerning spirit" which is a process of differentiating by the divine gift of a leader if a spirit is of God or not. Strategies for discerning disciples' or followers' needs can include the following:

Pay attention to your follower's specific needs. The servant must focus on the flock's needs without being prompted. These needs are as diverse as the people that have them and are often unique, dynamic, and not shared by others. Some of the needs might be intense or moderate; others might be temporary or permanent. The leader needs to know when the flock needs healing, when they are hungry, if the necessity is physical and spiritual, and if they are backsliding from the faith. Whatever these need might be; the leader must discern what need must be met as part of discipleship. This is where the leader-servant needs the spirit of discernment. He must be willing to give up his comfort and make the right sacrifices to disciple the followers. Some followers may need to grow spiritually, whereas some may be new members, nonbelievers, immature, or backslidden Christians. God's purpose and plan for each local church or fellowship are unique, requiring each leader-servant to discover what God's purpose is for the fellowship.

Nurture and develop the growth of assets of your followers. Recognizing the level of maturity and the assets of each follower is followed by efforts to nurture the desired growth in individuals. The leader must recognize that God has sanctified him and made him accountable as a shepherd to help the members of the church or organization to become what God wants him or her to be. The leader cannot afford to overemphasize unity or individual needs and minimize the collective need of the community. Such an approach will lead to conformity. Individuals will tend to conform to a narrower view of growth. Rather, the leader-servant must reconcile the needs of the individuals with what will transform the larger community. The goal of discipleship is to help the individual to be a leader who multiplies the growth of the organization. He must work to understand where everyone is in his or her faith and work with God to capitalize on the identified strength as a baseline for growth. If a member has the gift to vocalize, then create an opportunity for the person to join the singing group; if talent is found in teaching, create an opportunity to lead Bible study to maximize that talent, and so on.

Maximize each follower's use of his or her assets. Talent is one of the innate elements given by God of an individual's assets and one that can determine the effective use of acquired skills. However, talent is not everything and can be enriched to maximize its use in the service of others. How can a leader develop and maximize the talent of each follower? One strategy comes from John C. Maxwell's book, *Talent is Never Enough,* which noted that success is gained by teaching followers to make choices that will add value to the talent they have. He referred to such a person as a "Talent-Plus" person. [13] According to John C. Maxwell, Talent-Plus persons maximize their talents, reach their potential, and fulfill their destinies by adding purpose-driven choices such as beliefs, passion, initiative, focus, courage, and so on to their talent. For example, adding passion to your talent will energize the talent, or adding focus to your abilities to teach will direct that talent to a better course.

A leader-servant must not only develop the talents of everyone assigned to him; he must lead them to maximize the use of those talents. More than 50% of all CEOs of Fortune 500 Companies had a

C or C- average in their college studies, and 65% of all U.S. senators came from the bottom half of their school classes. Seventy-five percent of U.S. presidents were also in the lower-half club in school. And, more than 50% of millionaire entrepreneurs never finished college.[13] Talent is a God-given gift; everyone has it and has been sanctified (set aside) for it (Jeremiah 1:5). Leaders must help followers develop and maximize the identified talent each has more than the skills he or she wants.

Developing talents is a good goal. Nevertheless, an inordinate goal is to maximize the talent you have for the destiny you need to fulfill. This is what has created great leaders such as Bill Gates of Microsoft. I believe that a person who follows purpose-driven choices and puts 100% effort to maximize 20% of his or her talent has a considerable probability to reach his or her potential more quickly and to fulfill his or her destiny.

Enrich the life purpose of the follower

One question to ask a follower is what will best meet their purpose in life? Seek the answer by looking for life-focus issues such as walking with God, service to others, reverence, praise, and service to God. The servant must turn to God and trust Him to help identify what the needs are and the best way to meet them. Focusing on life issues may reveal some character flaws that need to be resolved. A prospective leader who cannot lead his family obviously needs to be trained in how he can be more faithful to his first responsibility. Correctly aligning the defined purpose of a potential talent with training the character qualities will help him realize his purpose, which will result in better equipping that leader for effective service.

Our children are our first followers to enrich their lives through fatherly discipleship. Dr. Jack Daniel and Omari Daniel in their book [14] *We Fish: The Journey to Fatherhood* presented an example of how we can enrich our personal life purpose and those of our loved ones. In observation, while fishing with Omari, Dr. Daniel reflected on the life he had, with his own father, and the cherished moments he spent with his daddy fishing. "I got so much out of fishing with Daddy during those precious summers that I was much better prepared for his death than I otherwise would have been...When we fished, I sometimes felt as though I was taking my son, not my daddy fishing. I loved teaching my father to fish, but I wanted my daddy to tell me where to cast. I wanted my daddy to cause the formal walls of father and son to fall and let us just be us."

Our life purpose and the purpose of those around us often depend on what we commit to and what we are willing to invest, and the time we have—admittedly, it is limited. We must therefore take advantage of every moment of our short time on earth to invest in the purpose to which God has called us. In my journey to fatherhood, when my only son was growing up, I was overly busy pursuing my education and career and spent little time with him alone to really get to know him beyond family devotion times and working on computers. As a result, during his college years, when I wanted to get close and bond with him, it was too late. We could not find anything we both could like and do together. I could not attach myself enough to him because I had lost the initial fertile period when he needed me to be most bonded to him as the only other man in the home. The little he learned from me working on computers became an inspiration and a pathway to his career today. Nevertheless, I wanted a strong father-and-son relationship. We love each other, but that love and relationship would be further enriched if I had invested a little more time into it—a lesson for any father reading these texts.

Pay attention to the needs of the community

A leader-servant is accountable to the community he serves. Equipping a follower for service must also include knowledge of how to manage the community. Diversity within an organization creates opportunities for creative and innovative ideas for growth. However, since the community is also made of diverse needs and challenges, overseeing the community of believers as part of discipleship involves overseeing the collective actions of the individuals and community as a whole.

Two extreme behaviors can occur as the leader tries to manage the community. First, he can overemphasize the group's diversity and minimize the assets (strengths, interests, and uniqueness) of each individual. The most likely outcome of this scenario is fragmentation or conflicts as individuals whose assets are neglected will feel less valued and empowered. Such individuals will not be fully engaged in their growth and will develop a sense of, "there is nothing for me."

Chapter 5
Developing the Acts of Attentive Discipleship

Second, the leader can overemphasize unity or the needs of individuals and minimize the collective needs of the community. The most likely outcome, in this case, will be conformity, as individuals strive to submit to whatever is prevalent in the community. This leads to a monoculture or unity of purpose. This is good if the organization is performing at its highest level. However, it does not allow for innovation and integration new ideas in managing skills. In this case, individuals will not grow beyond their talents, which will lead to stagnation. If the desired goal is to develop a leader-servant of high repute and upright standing, neither of these two extremes leads to the longed-for goal. Instead, merging its thriving Christian community goals with the trained assets of its potential leaders or elders will yield to the community externally known for its integrated inclusiveness and relationship toward service to others. Both the individuals and the organization grow.

I can state with a decent degree of confidence based on my years of experience that you cannot expect a strong fellowship or organization when there is no relationship between the members. You cannot expect to build good relationships when individuals harbor anger and are unforgiving. Nor can you expect a thriving fellowship that caters to the community it serves when individuals who make up that community are not fully committed to or engaged in the fellowship's mission. The leader-servant in discipleship must focus on the community as one body with many members and gifts. Such gifts include wisdom, knowledge, faith, healing, working miracles, prophecy, and the ability to distinguish between spirits, tongues, and interpretation of tongues. All of these skills are empowered by the same Spirit who apportions to each person individually as He wills. The success and effectiveness of a community to accomplish its God-given mission can be measured by the strengths and commitments of each member of the community to the shared vision of the organization. No member can be left out for being weak because; "God has so composed the body, giving greater honor to the part that lacked it… but that the members may have the same care for one another. If one member suffers, all suffer together; if one member is honored, all rejoice together" (1 Corinthians 12:24-25, NIV). This is a mindset and a principle that when applied to organizations in general will yield a culture of excellence in which the least and the greatest reach beyond their potential—just by sharing the use and distribution of the strength of the community

Other ways to facilitate group discipleship to maximize the strength of the community include creating and encouraging participation in group activities; building consensus among individuals; peer mentoring between individuals; creating a community of leaders; letting "iron-to sharpen iron" by creating one-on-one- mentoring relationships; generating a shared vision; using a culturally relevant communication strategy, such as celebrating national days; and weaving partnerships and networks with related organizations with similar mission connections.

SUMMARY 5
DEVELOPING THE ACTS OF ATTENTIVE DISCIPLESHIP

Before starting this exercise, please read and follow the instruction in the preface of this workbook. Answers to these questions are contained in this chapter. Completion of these exercises after reading the chapter should take 60-90 minutes.

Discovering the Acts of Attentive Discipleship

1. Define attentive discipleship
2. Attentive commitment calls for giving younger new followers the type of near observation newborn needs. Why is this important in a community made up of older and younger followers?.

Understanding the Principle of Attentive Discipleship

1. A person who follows purpose-driven choices and puts 100% effort to maximize 20% of his or her talent has a considerable probability to reach his or her potential more quickly and to fulfill his or her destiny.
    a. .[13] Talent is a God-given gift; everyone has it and has been sanctified (set aside) for it (Jeremiah 1:5). Why and how is talent not enough to develop a follower?

Chapter 5
Developing the Acts of Attentive Discipleship

2. Principle of attentive discipleship: No member can be left out for being weak as shown in the passage below.

   "God has so composed the body, giving greater honor to the part that lacked it… but that the members may have the same care for one another. If one member suffers, all suffer together; if one member is honored, all rejoice together" (1 Corinthians 12:24-25, NIV).
   a. What is the impact of this mindset and aprinciple when applied to organizations in general?
   b. How can you measure the strength of such an organization or group of diverse people?

Practicing the Acts of Attentive Discipleship

1. **Attentive Discipleship**- involves giving close attention to nurturing spiritual growth in others as a mother nurtures a newborn.
   a. How can you discern the needs of your disciples?
   b. How do you determine the needs of others?
   c. What are the desired outcomes of discipleship?
2. Paying attention to your follower's specific needs is an act of attentive discipleship. What must be the primary role or strategies in this case?
3. How can you nurture and develop the growth of assets of your followers?
4. Maximizing each follower's use of his or her assets reproduces skills. Talent is one of the innate elements given by God of an individual's assets. How can Talent determine the effective use of acquired skills.
5. How can the life purpose of the follower be enriched? Our children are our first followers to enrich their lives through fatherly discipleship. Consider the example of Dr. Jack Daniel and Omari Daniel in their book [14] *We Fish:*

   > *The Journey to Fatherhood presented an example of how we can enrich our personal life purpose and those of our loved ones. In observation, while fishing with Omari, Dr. Daniel reflected on the life he had, with his own father, and the cherished moments he spent with his daddy fishing. "I got so much out of fishing with Daddy during those precious summers that I was much better prepared for his death than I otherwise would have*

been...*When we fished, I sometimes felt as though I was taking my son, not my daddy fishing. I loved teaching my father to fish, but I wanted my daddy to tell me where to cast. I wanted my daddy to cause the formal walls of father and son to fall and let us just be us.*"

a. What can you learn from this story about our life purpose or that of our followers?
b. What happened to love and relationship when quality time and attention are shared during earlier life years with your child?
c. How can attentive disciple be managed in the context of a diverse community?

CHAPTER 6
Developing the Acts of Reproductive Discipleship

The desired outcome of discipleship is to reproduce Christ-likeness in the disciples whereby they emulate the principles and values of the shepherd. How did Jesus disciple or train His disciples so effectively that in less than three years, they learned and understood the message from Jesus (Luke 6:40)? Jesus' reproductive discipleship produced in His disciples all the principles he wanted to continue to teach and live by when He was gone. The Apostle Paul without doubt closely emulated the life of Christ. In equipping and building disciples to follow Christ-likeness, where do we start in the process to grow talents and develop new ones to build a thriving Christian community? In light of Paul's emphasis on character development, how do leaders train and equip others to serve with high integrity and remain above reproach? Understanding new believers' level of maturity to be a disciple will guide the leader in developing an appropriate Bible study series or training. The needs of disciples will have to be identified and corrected through sound teaching. Here are a few strategies to consider starting with individual disciples to the whole community of disciples or leaders as a unit:

Guide your disciple to discover personal purposes

Jesus used a type of teacher-guided, inquiry-based, discovery learning method that involved a four-stage process: [15]
  (1) Inspiring learners by identifying teachable moments,
  (2) Guiding inquiry with intriguing questions,
  (3) Allowing learners to explore hypotheses, and
  (4) Encouraging application.

Information a disciple discovers about him- or herself adds more value to the disciple's knowledge. For example, if one discovers that he or she can lead a small-group Bible study, it will motivate the person to want to develop more skills in that area.

Creating opportunities to discover more truth about the Word of God and themselves, the leader needs to know the personal purpose of the disciple. This then means that part of our reproductive discipleship activity is to include activities for teachable moments. This was one of Jesus' discovery learning strategies. Strategies to guide the disciple to discover personal purpose using teachable moments include the following.

Know your disciples and followers

A leader-servant knows his disciples and the followers and understands how to take advantage of situations as teaching moments. For example, in Matthew 9:4-5, Jesus used the question some teachers of the laws asked him about blasphemy to teach them that He had the power, not only to perceive their thoughts but to forgive sin and heal the sick. He used the signs He was performing as teachable moments; "Now while he was in Jerusalem at the Passover Festival, many people saw the signs he was performing and believed in his name " (John 2:23, NIV).

It was also a teachable moment when the disciples saw Jesus praying and asked Him; "Lord, teach us to pray, just as John taught his disciples" (Luke 11:1-2). And, Jesus also taught the disciples on being "full of faith" when Jesus reached out and caught the drowning Peter (Matthew 14:31). In each case, Jesus perceived the learners' or followers' readiness and curiosity to learn or discover something about themselves and used that effectively to communicate a truth. Another teachable moment that made many believe in Him was when Jesus raised dead Lazarus from the dead. "But I said this for the benefit of the people standing here, that they may believe that you sent me" (John 10:42).

Most of Jesus' actions were based on life situations, and He used every one of them as a teaching moment. That was very effective because He used the little that people knew and the questions, they asked to know what they did not know. He then used the questions He asked to expose their emotions to teach them the critical truth they needed to know. It is a classic example of discovery learning because people are personally engaged in the learning process. He had a way of making His stewards desire to discover more new truths. For example, Jesus led Peter to discover his pride when He refused to let the Lord wash his feet (Luke 10:28). He made the woman in the well know what "living water" was (John 4:10) or the desire for eternal life: "Teacher," he asked; "what must I do to inherit eternal life?" (Matthew 19:16, NKJV). He also used this technique to teach lessons about how to love the Lord and answer the question "Who is my neighbor?" Here, he taught about compassion using the Parable of the Good Samaritan (Luke 10: 25-37). In each case, the disciple discovered the truth for himself.

Use exploratory questions to guide discovery

As a Physics professor for the first 12 years of my career, I did not see any way to teach physics better than a teacher-directed, inquiry-based teaching and learning model. One of the critical elements of inquiry-based teaching/learning is using questions to explore reasoning, explain hypotheses, engage students in their learning, and guide the personal discovery of answers. Although it could be frustrating to the students, it usually lends itself to better retention of the material. In his book, *Extraordinary Results from Ordinary Teachers*, Michael D. Warden, founder, and president of Ascent Coaching Group, Inc., showed that Jesus was very effective in using this method of teaching.[16] We learned from the Gospels that Jesus used inquiry-based or discovery illumination very effectively to teach his followers, framing his questions and answers around parables and proverbs (maxims). The five most common ones indicated by Warden include:

(1) **Contrast.** A proverb that contrasts one thing with Another Do not store up for yourselves treasures on earth,…But store up for yourselves treasures in heaven"(Matthew 6:19-20)

(2) **Enigma.** Purposefully vague or obscure in order to challenge students to think: "Wherever there is a carcass, there the vultures will gather" (Matthew 24:28).

(3) **Humor.** A proverb that presents truth in a way that seems ludicrous or unexpected: "It is easier for a camel to go through the eye of a needle than for someone who is rich to enter the kingdom of God" (Matthew 19:24).

(4) **Metaphor.** This is a proverb that compares two people or things by directly equating them. "You are the light of the world. A town built on a hill cannot be hidden" (Matthew 5:14).

(5) Paradox. A proverb that appears to sound contradictory but is not: "Whoever finds their life will lose it, and whoever loses their life for my sake will find it" (Matthew 10:39).

Commission the followers to go and multiply

Multiplication is the most important and expected result of effective discipleship, which Jesus established in the Great Commission: "Therefore go and make disciples of all nations, baptizing them in the name of the Father and of the Son and of the Holy Spirit" (Matthew 28:18-20, NIV). A disciple must make other disciples in multiplicity more than in an additive sense. For example, if one disciple ministers to 100 persons, and each of these ministers to 100 persons, a total of 10,000 persons will be reached. Jesus knew the multiplicative power of discipleship, and Paul followed the same example. To the Thessalonians believers Paul wrote, "And so you became a model to all the believers in Macedonia and Achaia. The Lord's message rang out from you not only in Macedonia and Achaia—your faith in God has become known everywhere (1 Thessalonians 1:7-8, NIV).

STRATEGIES TO COMMISSION DISCIPLES

Charge the followers to extend their influence for greater growth. Paul charged the believers in Colossae (both Jews and Gentiles) saying, "In the same way, the gospel is bearing fruit and growing throughout the whole world…" (Colossians 1:6, NIV). Here, Paul was acknowledging the effect of the work of his disciples. After all, has been done and growth realized, you must step out to practice. Paul said the new knowledge in Christ must continue to bear fruit throughout the world by showing others what has been learned, who God is, and what Christ-likeness means to them. Trained disciples must learn to extend their knowledge outside themselves and expand themselves outside their circle of friends and fellowships. This is also a way of holding them accountable for what they have learned. It is equally important as a powerful way to motivate them to avoid stagnation as they continue to focus on fruit beyond themselves. Some churches and organizations today die when leaders fail to reach out beyond themselves. In the Great Commission by Jesus (Matthew 28), when you misunderstand the meaning of "your Jerusalem," how can you understand the uttermost part of the World? An organization loses its significance when it fails to reach its original purpose within a greater commission outside itself. The vision that keeps an organization from stagnation or produces a great organization is the vision that is bigger than the organization itself.

Create opportunities for practice of all that they have learned. Commissioning the disciples is a way of encouraging them to apply what they have learned to make other disciples for the Kingdom's business. Disciples are also to practice what they preach. Jesus concluded the Parable of the Good Samaritan with "Go and do likewise" (Matthew 10:37, NIV) He was telling the disciples that now that they know who a good neighbor is and his complete compassionate empathy in sharing in the suffering of others, they should follow the same example. He called the Pharisees "hypocrites" because they did not practice what they preached in reciting the laws of Moses (Matthew 23:2-7). In the same way, Paul encouraged his followers to "Keep putting into practice all you learned and received from me—everything you heard from me and saw me doing. Then the God of peace will be with you" (Philippians 4:19, NLT). To put into practice means to live out the example of what you have been taught and to teach others the same. The learning is of no effect and will not be retained for long unless the disciple increases in knowledge and is willing to apply that knowledge to new situations. When Jesus sent out the 70, He wanted them to use what they had learned. In the words of John C. Maxwell, "preparation positions your talent" and "practice sharpens your talent." [17] You become perfect in using your talent or skill by continuously practicing that talent in different contexts. Paul charged Timothy to follow his teaching as a way of life, purpose, faith, patience, and love; enduring persecutions and sufferings and to learn how the Lord rescued him (2 Timothy 3:10-11). This is Paul's excellent transparent attempt to reproduce in this young leader everything about him, including his suffering and source of strength. He shared the same and more with his other disciple, Titus (Titus 2:7-8).

Prepare the follower for contingencies

No matter how much you plan or disciple someone, in the mission field, things do not always proceed as planned. Planning for the "out of a plan" situation is your contingency against the possible unknowns. It is difficult to predict what might happen at any time, but one can always plan for variations. For example, in church planting or bringing a fresh gospel message to an unknown neighborhood, one should plan for the social issues that might arise as a result of a new message. On mission trips, not planning for medical emergencies in the case someone gets sick could result in terminating the mission. Jesus, in sending out his disciples, provided a good example. He was aware of things that could create surprise or teachable moments. In planning against those, He gave the disciples the following specific instructions on what they needed to do in the cases that might arise:

(1) Submit to the authority of Jesus even when challenged. Such submission allows them to remain focused on the Lord's agenda. As leaders, we are to expect that things can go wrong. Our authority can be challenged, but we must remain focused on what the Lord has taught.
(2) Do not be afraid of people's intentions. Do not be frightened if you are called something you know you are not; fear only Jesus, because people's intentions will be revealed. Practice what you have learned because you reproduce what you can learn from the Lord.
(3) Do not be discouraged by the overwhelming needs that might arise in the field. When those needs arise, trust Him who sent you for support and strength; "You are of more value than many sparrows" (Matthew 10:31, NKJV).
(4) Be humble before men even when you are challenged; otherwise, you will be rejected by God.
(5) The message will be difficult for some to accept and will divide families and friends against friends; you must take your own cross as a personal sacrifice.
(6) Your message will bring blessings; those who extend help to you will be blessed.

SUMMARY 6
DEVELOPING THE ACTS OF REPRODUCTIVE DISCIPLESHIP

Before starting this exercise, please read and follow the instruction in the preface of this workbook. Answers to these questions are contained in this chapter. Completion of these exercises after reading the chapter should take 60-90 minutes.

Discovering Acts of Reproductive Discipleship

1. Define Reproductive Discipleship.
2. How did Jesus model reproductive discipleship? What was the results (Luke 6:40)?
3. In equipping and building disciples to follow Christ-likeness, where do we start in the process to grow talents and develop new ones to build a thriving Christian community?
4. Considering Paul's emphasis on character development, how do leaders train and equip others to serve with high integrity and remain above reproach?
    a.

Understanding the Principle of Reproductive Discipleship

1. How did Jesus demonstrate the principle of multiplication Spirit" (Matthew 28:18-20, NIV).
2. Jesus knew the multiplicative power of discipleship. How did Apostle Paul in 1 Thessalonians 1:7-8, NIV).

Practicing the Acts of Reproductive Discipleship

1. Guiding your disciple to discover personal purposes was discussed as one strategy. How did Jesus use teacher-guided, inquiry-based, discovery learning method[15] Fill in the blanks:
    a. Inspiring learners by _____ teachable moments,
    b. Guiding inquiry with _____ questions,
    c. Allowing learners to _____ hypotheses, and
    d. _____ application.

2. How did following strategies based om life situation guide the disciple to discover personal purpose using teachable moments . (Matthew 19:16, NKJV). (Luke 10: 25-37).
    a. Know your disciples and followers. What did the disciple discover about the truth for themselves in the following passages: .
        i. Matthew 9:4-5, (John 2:23, NIV).
        ii. (Luke 11:1-2).
        iii. (Matthew 14:31, John 10:42; Luke 10:28).
    b. Use exploratory questions to guide discovery Jesus was very effective in using this method of teaching. [16] framing his questions and answers around parables and proverbs (maxims). The five most common ones showed by Warden[16] (see Matthew 6:19-20; Matthew 24:28; Matthew 19:24; Matthew 5:14; and Matthew 10:39).
3. To commission the followers to go and multiply, how was the principle of multiplication important and expected result of effective discipleship?
4. To charge the followers to extend their influence for greater growth as a strategy for reproduction. (Colossians 1:6, NIV), what was Apostle doing in this passage?
5. In the Great Commission by Jesus (Matthew 28), how did Jesus Create opportunities for practice of all that they have learned? (Matthew 10:37, NIV)
6. How did Apostle Paul encourage his followers reproduce? Philippians 4:19, NLT). How is is true in the John C. Maxwell, "preparation positions your talent" and "practice sharpens your talent."[17] see also 2 Timothy 3:10-11, Titus (Titus 2:7-8).
7. How did Jesus Prepare the follower for contingencies and challenges associated with multiplication in reproductive discipleship (Matthew 10:31, NKJV).
8. Take the Leadership Influence attribute audit in Table 2.
9. Based on the questions in Table 2. can you identify each of the acts of discpleship leadership attribute? What ones did you score 3 ("sometimes") or less than 3? Review and learn and commit to work to improve

Table 12.3 Leadership Discipleship Attribute Audit

Servant leadership discipleship attribute is the combined acts of personally developing, intentionally equipping, and attentively empowering growth in others to reproduce a heart of service. Assess the quality of your acts of discipleship attribute by inserting an X below the number that best describes your response to each statement.

Item	Acts of Affection Attribute Check 1= Always; 2= Frequently; 3= Sometimes; 4= Almost Never; 5= Never	1	2	3	4	5
1	I develop followers by one-on-one engagement					
2	I personally mentor, equip, and empower growth and heart of service in others					
3	I show followers a pattern to follow to model their lives					
4	I develop followers to become great leaders					
5	I make deliberate selfless act to motivate others					
6	My intentional acts of discipleship are purposefully directed to equip followers for growth					
7	I guard the followers against false teachings from within or outside					
8	I give close attention to nurture the spiritual growth in others.					
9	I am usually able to discern and determine the needs of the followers					
10	I create opportunities to encourage followers to practice what they know or have learned.					
	Add up your rating in each column					
Total Score	Guide and Explanation of Score: understand the areas you need to further develop	Total				
10-17	Great discipleship leader; keep it up!
18-25	Above Average discipleship; need to work 25% of the areas
26-33	Average but developing; need to work on 50% of the areas
34-41	Below average discipler, need to work on 75% of the key areas
42-50	Not discipleship attribute; need to work in all the areas

TOPIC INDEX

About This Book, 22
Affective Compassion, 73, 78
Attentive commitment, 78
Attentive discipleship, 59, 79
authentic, 24, 26
authentic leadership, 37, 95
Authentic Leadership, 45, 94, 95
Authenticity, 43
Comfort, 41
commitment, 19, 25
Comparisons
  with other works, 40
contingency, 88
Contrast
  maxims, 85
credibility, 48
Discerning needs, 73
Discipleship
  definition of, 27, 53
discipleship outward attribut, 56
discipleship *reproduces*, 56
distinguishes
  a leader's act of giving, 29
empowers, 55
Enigm
  maxims, 85
Follow the Master, 54
Functional Definitions, 35
Generosity
  definition of, 29
Generosity c, 29
giving, 29, 59, 79
  habit of, 29
Great Commission, 86, 90
Humor
  maxims, 85
inside-out, 46
intentional discipleship
  in spiritual discipleship, 59, 69
Joshua, 19
law of, 42
Leader as Servant Leadership, 42
  definition, 25

Leader First., 23
Leader-as-Servant Leadership, 23
leader-servant's affection-attribute
  definition, 48, 56
leadership, **25**
Leadership Attributes, 43
Leadership Inner Value system, 25
life purpose, 75, 76, 79, 80
Metaphor.
  maxims, 85
Model, 23
Moses, 19
Multiplicatio, 86
multiplicative power, 89
Navigation-attribute, 48
Intentionality, 67
Nurture and develop the growth, 74
Organizational leadership trust, 32
Paradox.
  maxims, 86
Personal Outward Authenticity, 47
Principle of attentive discipleship, 79
Principle of Attentive Discipleship, 78
process, 25
Self-deny yourself, 54
Servant, 23, 24
Servant leadership discipleship
  attribute, 56, 58
shepherding skills, 55
shepherds, 55
spiritual discipleship, 56, 58, 61, 67, 69
Spiritual Discipleship, 61
State the additive law of discipleship, 58
Strategies for Intentional Discipleship,
  67
suffering, 59, 91
Take up your cross daily, 54
teachable moment, 84
test
  for leader-servant authenticity, 46
  of essential elements of personal authenticity,
    46, 47
The Leadership Influence-attribute, 41

REFERENCES

Greenleaf, R. (1970). *The Servant as Leader,* Indianapolis: The Robert K. Greenleaf Center

Spears, L. (1996). *"Reflections on Robert K. Greenleaf and servant-leadership."* Leadership & Organization Development Journal, 17(7), 33-35

Russell, R.F. (2001). "The role of values in servant leadership." *Leadership & Organization Development Journal,* 22(2), 76-83

Russell, R.F., and Stone, A.G. (2002). "A review of servant leadership attributes: developing a practical model." *Leadership & Organization Development Journal,* 23(3), 145-15

Terry. R. W (1993). *Authentic Leadership: Courage In Action,* San Francisco, CA Jossey-Bass

George, B (2003). *Authentic Leadership: Rediscovering the Secrets to Creating Lasting Value.* San Francisco, CA, Jossey-Bass

Shamir, B. & Eilam, G. (2005). "What's your story? Toward a life-story approach to authentic leadership." Leadership Quarterly, 16, 395–418.

Anderson, GL (2009). Advocacy Leadership: Toward a Post-Reform Agenda in Education, Routledge, New York, 41

Yacobi, B.G. *"Elements of Human Authenticity."* http://www.philosophytogo.org/wordpress/?p=1945, Retrieved, July 15, 2012

George, B (2003). *Authentic Leadership: Rediscovering the Secrets to Creating Lasting Value,* San Francisco, CA, Jossey-Bass

Wosu, SN (2014), *Leader as Servant Leadership Model,* Xulon Press

González, MP, Barrull, E; Ponsy, C, and Marteles, P, (1998]. *"What is Affection?"* http://www.biopsychology.org/biopsychology/papers/what_is_affection.html

Maxwell, JC (2007).*Talent is Never Enough,* Thomas Nelson

Daniel, J and Daniel, O (2003), *We Fish: The Journey to Fatherhood,* University of Pittsburgh Press. 197

Lee, HeeKap "Jesus Teaching Through Discovery", *A Journal of the International Christian Community for Teacher Education*, Volume 1, Number 2: http://icctejournal.org/issues/v1i2/v1i2-lee/. Retrieved June 12, 2013:

Warden, M.D (1998). *Extraordinary Results from Ordinary Teachers*, Group Pub Inc.

Maxwell, JC (2007).*Talent is Never Enough* , Thomas Nelson